INTO THE
PSALMS

INTO THE
PSALMS

Verses for the Heart
Music for the Soul

INTO THE PSALMS

© 2015 by Dr. Rolan Monje and Illumination Publishers
ISBN: 978-1-941988-10-7

Unless otherwise noted, all Scripture quotations are from the *Holy Bible, New International Version* (NIV), copyright © 1973, 1978, 1984, by International Bible Society.

Scripture quotations marked ESV are from *The Holy Bible, English Standard Version*, copyright © 2011 by Crossway Bibles.

Scripture quotations marked NAB are from the *New American Bible*, copyright © 1970, 1986, 1991 by Confraternity of Christian Doctrine.

Scripture quotations marked NASB taken from the *New American Standard Bible®*, Copyright © 1960, 1962, 1963, 1968, 1971, 1972, 1973, 1975, 1977, 1995 by The Lockman Foundation Used by permission." (www.Lockman.org)

Scripture quotations marked NRSV are from the *New Revised Standard Version of the Bible*, copyright © 1989 by the Division of Christian Education of the National Council of the Churches of Christ in the USA.

Scriptures marked NLT are taken from *Holy Bible, New Living Translation*, copyright © 1996, 2004, 2007 by Tyndale House Foundation. Used by permission of Tyndale House Publishers Inc. All rights reserved.

Scripture quotations marked TEV are from *Good News Bible: The Bible in Today's English Version*, copyright © 1966, 1971, 1976 by the American Bible Society.

Scripture quotations marked KJV are from *The Holy Bible, King James Version*.

Cover design by Bing Bernardo-Gaw. Printed in the United States of America by Illumination Publishers.

About the author: Serving as evangelist and teacher, Dr. Rolan Monje has taught in various settings in North America, Indochina, the Middle East, and the Asia-Pacific regions. He holds degrees from the University of the Philippines (BS), the University of London (BD), and the American Bible College-Florida (MMin, DMin). His graduate studies converge mainly on biblical theology and languages—Hebrew, Greek and Aramaic. Rolan and his wife, Weng, have been involved in teaching and counseling ministries for over two decades. They have two daughters, Yana and Stefi. They serve with the Metro Manila Christian Church in Manila, Philippines.

ILLUMINATION IP
PUBLISHERS

www.ipibooks.com
6010 Pinecreek Ridge Court
Spring, Texas 77379-2513

Dedication

To Weng –
the bride of my youth,
my dearest gift from God.

With you, life is a joyous duet.

CONTENTS

CONTENTS

Part Three: Into Our Lifes

Foreword

It is a privilege to write the foreword for this book. Not only is it a valuable addition to the literature that helps us understand one of the longest book in the Bible, it is written by one of my closest friends and co-workers, Dr. Rolan Monje. Psalms is a treasure chest for scholar and ordinary Christian alike. It is both imminently practical and deeply theological. No wonder it is the most quoted Old Testament book in the New Testament.

Rolan correctly observes that most of the Bible is a record of God speaking to and about man, whereas Psalms is more a record of man speaking to God. Yet, since those speaking (or singing) to God did so by inspiration of the Holy Spirit, the theological truths are valid.

When interpreting the Bible, understanding context is everything. Imagine receiving a letter and opening it without looking to see who sent it or to whom it is addressed. Further, imagine taking out page five of a twelve page letter and reading one sentence from the middle of the page. Do you think that would be a valid way to grasp the contents of the letter? Of course not, you say. Yet, many pull isolated statements out of a biblical passage with little or no attention to either the context of the book or of the passage itself.

The five poetic books of the Old Testament are not always easy to interpret contextually. The book of Proverbs gives us the most difficulty in determining context, because the majority of it contains a mixture of topics within almost every chapter. Thus it is often called a "string of pearls" style of writing. The Psalms are easier to interpret contextually, simply because each psalm has a specific context. Rolan's book helps the untrained eye to see the various connections within Psalms, thus helping us understand the value of context to become much more proficient at dealing with it. For example, he shows that there is a general progression in the Psalms as a whole — from lament to thanksgiving to praise, in what he calls a "life application" sequence.

The Psalms speak much more to the heart than to the mind, for they arise from the basic human needs of the writers. Rolan presents different ways to group the Psalms—for example, categorizing them according to emotions and needs. He also gives some very practical directions and examples about how to interpret each psalm, and includes chapters on the God of the Psalmists, the Messianic Psalms, the Imprecatory Psalms (those calling down curses on enemies), and a guide to meditation. In reading this book, you will indeed get "into the Psalms" as the title promises, and in so doing, you will get more out of the Psalms than ever before.

Rolan's in-depth explanations and practical directions are excellent. You will get to know his heart for God, his family, and his friends as you engage his writing. His intellect, knowledge, and writing skills are equally matched by his humility, an all-too-rare combination.

Once you start reading this book, you will not want to put it down until you have plumbed its depths. You will find yourself reading with Bible open and a notepad or computer nearby as you will want to record thoughts, questions, and applications to your own heart.

Thank you, my dear brother, for your life and your teaching in its various forms, especially now in this present form of the written word. You have blessed us!

—Gordon Ferguson
Dallas, Texas

Acknowledgements

The shaping of this book follows the course of my spiritual journey. It has been an exhilarating one, and along the way, I've been blessed with some great companions.

Any book project comes to fruition only with the help and encouragement of many. I wish to thank

- The Metro Manila Christian Church, especially Pasig Region, and the Visayan Family of Churches for your love and prayers. It's been great learning and growing together.

- Our fellowship of churches, the Philippine staff and church leaders, for your support.

- My fellow teachers for your reassurance and generous spirit. Special thanks to Tom Jones and Glenn Giles for your input on this book.

- Andre Publico, Paris Murray and Rommel Casis for your friendship and valuable ideas on the manuscript.

- Kat Corpus, Wendy Bayona and Enthrem Bagtas for editing and giving suggestions.

- Bing Bernardo-Gaw for the cover design.

- Gordon Ferguson, for being a wellspring of inspiration. You are both a mentor and friend. It has been a unique blessing to work with you and learn from you.

- My parents and extended family for never doubting my dreams.

- My wife, Weng, and daughters, Yana and Stefi, for your sincere belief in me. Weng, thank you for constantly being there for me throughout this project. Your deep devotion and unfailing interest in spiritual matters never fail to light my fire.

Preface

Whom have I in heaven but you?
  And earth has nothing I desire besides you...

I call with all my heart; answer me, O LORD...

My soul thirsts for God, for the living God.
  When can I go and meet with God?

These few excerpts from The Book of Psalms touch upon the essential fact that it is a book about relationship—having a real and meaningful connection with God. Far from dry and dreary religion, worship and prayer in the Psalms is spirited and sincere. The psalmists declare that all are *invited* to encounter God and to dialogue with him. That invitation comes down to us...and also led to this book being written.

This book is for anyone who wants to get *into the Psalms*. To help you on the way, my goal is to provide an overview of Psalms and equip you with tools for interpretation and life application. There are three parts:

- **Part One** is called *Into Their World*. The psalms are products of a socio-cultural setting dramatically different from our own. We must bridge this gap in order to appreciate them.

- **Part Two,** *Into Their Message*, expounds on the types of psalms and highlights the major themes, including Jesus in the Psalms. This segues into practical application.

- **Part Three,** *Into Our Lives*, emphasizes the psalms as valuable life-tools for living a life of praise. I end with learning helps for studying individual psalms, such as guidelines for working through the text, as well as a sample study.

Into the Psalms makes use of the New International Version (NIV), 1984 ed. and other translations found on the copyright page. Taken together or individually these translations embody much of the flavor suggested by Hebrew poetry without straying from the root meanings of the words. Other conventions worth mentioning are:

- In accordance with common usage "The Psalms," "Psalms," or "Psalter," with an uppercase "P" refers to the entire Book of Psalms, while lowercase "psalms" is for general use. Most English Bible versions entitle the anthology "(The) Psalms" (e.g., NIV, ASV, RSV, NASB, JB, NEB) or "The Book of Psalms" (KJV, NAB, NKJV).

- For simplicity sake, only the chapter and verse will be mentioned when referring to Psalms. Thus "(Psalm 19:14)" is simply "(19:14)." Other shortcuts: When explaining etymological roots, I abbreviate "Hebrew" as "Heb" and "Greek" as "Grk." "Verse/s" are "v" and "vv," respectively.

- For the Hebrew Text, I used the Masoretic Text preserved in the Westminster Leningrad Codex, the *Biblia Hebraica Stuttgartensia*.

- I use "the Lord" and "Yahweh" interchangeably for the personal name of God. This seemed wise to do, following convention, and without necessarily avoiding the issues associated with the *Tetragrammaton* ("The Four Letters") — YHWH.

- All italics used in quoted Scripture are my own and are for purposes of emphasis only.

- Excursus (digressions/detailed explanations) are included in the main text of the book for interested readers.

Technical terms have been kept to a minimum, except where they aid your understanding. For reference, a short glossary is provided at the end of the book.

I warmly welcome any and all feedback. I look forward to growing as a student of Scripture. *Soli Deo Gloria.*

—Rolan Monje
Manila, Philippines

Part One

Into Their World

O world, as God has made it! All is beauty.

—Robert Browning

The psalms are poems, and poems have meaning—although the poet has no obligation to make his meaning immediately clear to anyone who does not want to make an effort to discover it.

—Thomas Merton

Introduction

They called it *shir*.

Shir was expression. *Shir* was communication. *Shir*, in Hebrew, means "song."

Ancient Israel was a people of song. *Shir* was not just about exercising your vocal chords; it was about life. To sing was to be alive. To be alive was to sing. Moses well captures this propensity with the words, "Then Israel sang this song...."

It was common for the Israelites to respond to events with music, to interpret life with song. It is not hard to imagine that, after narrowly escaping Pharaoh's army, Israel breaks into singing. Moses leads the chorus and Miriam enters the scene with tambourines and dancing (Exodus 15). It is not surprising that fresh from a victorious military campaign, Deborah and Barak come up with a duet of praise (Judges 5). In addition, think about David's poetic lament for Saul and Jonathan (2 Samuel 1), Jonah's hymnic prayer while inside the fish (Jonah 2), and Isaiah's visionary song about Israel (Isaiah 5). Surely Israel had a taste for harmonizing life with music.

And don't we also?

Most everyone in the world sings—in the street, in the shower, in homes, in churches. We sing to celebrate occasions, to memorialize events, to honor those worthy, to remember those departed. We sing of success. We sing of failure. We sing from exhilaration as well as from boredom. We sing to let off steam. We sing to nurse broken hearts. Even those who can barely carry a tune, manage to whistle or hum.

In this sense, we are like the ancient Israelites.

Yet what makes Israel special is the spiritual dimension expressed through their music. Verse sprang from reflection, song from spirituality. The ancient artisans blended art and science, time and space, to create musical masterpieces which brilliantly reflected, above all, their faith. Verse and song point to God.

As providence would have it, God has given us those songs, biblical texts that engage Israel's musicality and ours: Psalms. Remarkably, a whole book of the Old Testament—one hundred and fifty chapters—is devoted to song. God knows people. He knows we are musical creatures.

It has been said that singing is the highest expression of music, perceived as the most direct expression of the emotions of the soul. If so, then Psalms is the most personal of the books of the Bible. In composing the psalms, the psalmists bared their deepest sentiments and their most profound convictions. In reading these psalms, we recognize things deep within ourselves. Perhaps this is why Calvin called them "an anatomy of all the parts of the soul."

And so with all their truth and reality, the psalms come down through the centuries to offer themselves to be read, understood and appreciated.

May these ancient songs—verses for the heart, music for the soul—resonate in us, just as they have done for readers throughout the ages.

Chapter One

Songs of Great Worth

By day the LORD commands his steadfast love,
and at night his song is with me,
a prayer to the God of my life. —Psalm 42:8 NRSV

WHAT ARE PSALMS?

Psalms are songs. They are lyric poetry, musical poems from ancient Israel. Among the Hebrew terms applied to them are

shir, which means "song," and
mizmor, from the verb "to sing" or "make music."[1]

So psalms are musical compositions. They lend themselves to rhythms and melodies. We don't know exactly how they were sung in the past, but we know that they were chanted or somehow intoned. Many were interpreted according to tunes familiar to earlier congregations.

Psalms are prayers—*tephillot*, the Jews would say. They were words spoken by men to God. These one hundred and fifty prayers in poetic form were spoken by men, yet considered Scripture. Whereas most biblical literature is God's word to man, the Book of Psalms constitutes man's words to God. The psalms are Israel's prayers we are privileged to make our own.

Psalms are praises. Collectively, they were called "Book of Praises." They lift up God's great qualities and extol him for his mighty deeds. As products of a community of faith, they were used for individual worship, but mainly for group worship. And though they were written about three thousand years ago, their praises still ring.

The Importance of Psalms

If you flip open your printed Bible right in the center, you will likely land in Psalms. Although this simply goes as a result of book binding, it somehow illustrates the centrality of Psalms. These ancient poems explore the very core of man's relationship with God. They speak of what is central to faith.

To Jesus

Jesus was very familiar with the Psalter (another name for The Book of Psalms). Back then, his Bible was the Old Testament, which was translated into Greek from the original Hebrew. This Greek translation, called the Septuagint (or LXX) included the Psalms.

During his earthly ministry, Jesus prayed the psalms and recited from them often in his preaching. He used them to answer questions and to defend his ministry. Jesus referred to Psalms to show he was the fulfillment of prophecy. He even quoted from Psalms as he was dying on the cross!

Like other Jews, Jesus would sing psalms. After the Last Supper, Jesus and his disciples sang a *hymn* (Matthew 26:30). In that time, Jewish hymns were traditionally from the *Hallel* series, Psalms 114–118.[2]

Before his ascension, Jesus sought to leave his disciples with knowledge and conviction. One important teaching of his had to do with his identity as revealed in Scripture. To enlighten his disciples, Jesus says in Luke 24:44 that the Psalms talk about him.

> He said to them, "This is what I told you while I was still with you: Everything must be fulfilled that is written about me in the Law of Moses, the Prophets and the *Psalms*." Then he opened their minds so they could understand the Scriptures. (Luke 24:44-45)

To the Early Church

The first Christians took on the same appreciation of Psalms that Jesus had. They incorporated psalms in their prayer and worship. The Psalter was seen by the early church as a sort of hymnbook, much as ancient Israel saw it (1 Corinthians 14:26). In fellowship, Christians would preach and encourage each other from the Psalms. Remember when Paul and Silas were thrown into jail? The Bible says they were singing "the praises of God" (Acts 16:25), which most likely indicates the hymns of the Psalter.

Various New Testament writers attest to the wide use of psalms. Early in Acts, Luke talks about a crucial time of decision-making. In the ensuing discussion, Peter invoked Psalms 69 and 109 (Acts 1:20). At a later time, when James wrote to Jewish Christians, he said,

> Is anyone among you suffering? Let him pray. Is anyone cheerful? Let him sing *psalms*. (James 5:13)

Clearly the early church saw the singing of psalms as a spontaneous expression of joy. Elsewhere, Paul encouraged disciples to keep singing the psalms, affirming their importance for worship and personal spirituality.

> Let the word of Christ dwell in you richly in all wisdom, teaching and admonishing one another in *psalms and hymns and spiritual songs*, singing with grace in your hearts to the Lord. (Colossians 3:16 KJV)

> Speaking to one another in *psalms and hymns and spiritual songs*, singing and making melody in your heart to the Lord. (Ephesians 5:19 NASB)

Psalms is the Old Testament book that is most often quoted and alluded to in the New Testament. When making theological points, the New Testament writers cite 93 verses or sentences from the Psalms, some multiple times.[3] Psalms were used to present the gospel, particularly because they anticipate Jesus (e.g., Acts 13:33). Paul refers extensively to Psalms in his writings. The Letter to the Hebrews is almost a running dialogue with Psalms, citing passages to demonstrate the supremacy of Christ. In this way, Psalms makes a critical connection between the Old Testament and New Testament.

As a reflection of faith experience, The Psalms is a volume waiting to be read and absorbed. It is a book of great worth. There is much to glean and gain from these inspired poems. The more you read the psalms and learn about them, the more interesting they become.

What's in a Name?

If you look at the heading of Psalm 145, you will find this title:
A psalm of praise. Of David. The Hebrew word translated "psalm"
is *tehillah*. Its root means "praise." (You will hear the same root when
you pronounce the word "hallelujah.") The Hebrews referred to the
psalms as *tehillim* (praises), a term that reflects much of the book's
content.[4]

What about the English word *psalm*?

- We get *psalm* from the Greek word *psalmos*, which means "song."
  It can mean "a stringed instrument" or "a song sung to stringed
  accompaniment."[5]

- Plucked instrumentation was the typical background for ancient lyric poetry as words were sung or intoned. In time however, the word *psalmos* came to mean "song of praise" or simply
  "song," without reference to strings.[6]

- Luke uses *psalmos* in his gospel and in Acts when he terms the
  whole collection "the Book of Psalms" (Luke 20:42; Acts 1:20)
  and "The Psalms" (Luke 24:44). In later centuries, English trans-
  lators transliterated the plural form *psalmoi* from the Greek re-
  sulting in the title "Psalms" in English Bibles.

Digging Deeper

Psalms are universally well-loved. Something about the psalms'
ability to touch people makes them widely popular. Throughout the
centuries, people have read, sung and memorized the Psalter more
than any other book of the Bible. Today, most handy New Testaments
are bound along with Psalms.

Yet for all its popularity, Psalms can be a perplexing read. For
beyond the familiar lines in hymns, readings, posters and stickers, the
psalms may leave you wondering and unresolved. After a while, what
seems clear and understandable becomes hard to grasp. Countless
times I have jumped "into the pool" of Psalms and found myself deep
underwater, needing to come up for air. As I journal my thoughts on
Psalms, I join C. S. Lewis as one who feels that he is writing "learned"
about things in which he is "unlearned himself."

Moreover there are certain features in Psalms that seem to defy
interpretation:

Why do several psalms directly question God?

How is one to interpret long litanies of misery?

What are we to make of poems of Israel's history?

Or what about passages that seem repetitious?

Or what of lines that call curses upon enemies?

Because of their peculiar tone and cultural detachment, particular psalms are glossed over or altogether avoided. Many Christians prefer to stick with the more familiar ones such as Psalms 23, 1 and 100. Others begin the noble goal of reading through the Psalter, one by one, only to stop midway. Such things shouldn't stop us from getting the most from the psalms. We need to consider the blessings that come with studying *all* the psalms, even the unfamiliar ones.

The call for us is to dig deeper. We need to exert some energy to learn about the psalms. Sure it will take time, but the benefits eclipse the efforts. Great blessings and growth await us. Let's get into the psalms!

Summary Points

- The psalms are songs, praises, and prayers.
- The Greek word *psalmos* stands behind the titles we find in our modern Bibles.
- Some psalms might be familiar to us, but there is great benefit in learning about all the psalms.

Chapter Two

Background of Psalms

Your word, O LORD, is eternal;
it stands firm in the heavens.

— Psalm 119:89

IF PSALMS WERE A MOUNTAIN RANGE, they would be among the grandest. They cause you to marvel, presenting one breathtaking and emotional view after another.

But the big picture isn't all there is to see. There is more, but you have to get close and climb it, actually climb it. You have to get your gear on and lay your hands on rock and soil. Only in working your way up do you get to see the details. Then you have time to explore the cracks and crevices. Then you discover sights you might otherwise have missed.

This chapter gives you background material to prepare you to scale to the summit of Psalms. This is an overview, acquainting you with the setting, place in scripture, authorship, and layout of Psalms. We will also briefly tackle the types of psalms and their headings.

Setting

The psalms are generally associated with what is commonly referred to as the United Kingdom Period of Israel. This era (about 1100–950 BC) is sometimes referred to as the Golden Age of the Jewish nation. It saw the reign of their three most famous kings: Saul, David and Solomon. Prior to this time, Israel was a loose confederation of separate tribes. Everything changed when they asked for a king. The establishment of a monarchy led to national identity and the building of the temple. When worship was later centralized in Jerusalem, the temple became an important factor in the religious life of the nation.[7]

Worship in Israel

Shortly after Solomon gained the throne, the Temple became the hub of Israel's worship. As the centerpiece of reverence toward God, it was there that Jewish festivals were held and offerings carried out. Through David's musical legacy, singing was incorporated. Psalm 107 captures this phenomenon, declaring,

> Let them sacrifice thank offerings
> and tell of his works with songs of joy. (Psalm 107:22)

Note how the verse above combines the activities of sacrifice and song. It was in this fusion of ritual and music that psalms came to be integral.[8]

Psalms were composed to be sung as communal expressions of praise and joy (1 Chronicles 15:16; 23:5, 30). Even after the time of David, the psalms kept their place in the nucleus of worship.

- Psalms looked to a much brighter future for God's people, encouraging them to keep their faith in him (1 Chronicles 25:1, 3).

- During the reign of Solomon, psalms were caroled at the dedication of the temple (2 Chronicles 5:7–8).

- After the country divided into the Northern and Southern Kingdoms, the Psalms remained part of Jewish religious culture. Kings such as Hezekiah and Josiah made use of the Psalms (2 Chronicles 29:30; 35:15).

- Nehemiah upheld their use after the return from the Exile (Nehemiah 12:31–39).

Dating and Timelessness

Despite what we know about their general history, setting the individual psalms in a chronological timeline is much tougher. The psalms do not indicate when they were written. We can only make guesses from the text. Though, as explained earlier, most of the psalms share the broad setting of temple ritual, the *specific* historical occasions for each of the 150 psalms widely vary. The events which led to the composition of the psalms span the time period from the Exodus in the fourteenth century BC (Psalm 90) up to the exile to Babylon in the sixth century BC (Psalm 137). Dating the individual compositions is difficult, and in most cases impossible.

For those of us who are familiar with the steps of Bible interpretation, we know that delving into the historical background is one of the first steps to be taken. This is foundational before one applies Scriptures to real life. But what do you do with the evasive settings of the psalms? Fortunately for us, such challenges don't render the Bible irrelevant. The psalms, along with the rest of Scripture, continue to speak! We shall see that there is a timelessness about the psalms which allows readers to appreciate and apply their message in any age.

Place in Scripture

In the Christian Bible, the Old Testament books are commonly arranged in fourfold division:

- Law — 5 books
- Poetry — 5 books
- Histories — 12 books
- Prophets — 17 books

The Book of Psalms falls under the poetry category along with Job, Proverbs, Ecclesiastes and Song of Songs. Together, these five poetic books make for significant amounts of biblical material — a total of 243 chapters out of the 929 in the entire Old Testament. They are typically placed between Histories and Prophets, but this can be misleading since much poetic material figures in the Prophets as well. In order to better understand the book of Psalms, one has to understand its place in the *Hebrew* Bible.

The Hebrew Bible

The Jews have a very different way of arranging Old Testament material. They recognize three divisions: the *Torah*, meaning "law" or "instruction," the *Nevi'im*, meaning "prophets," and *Kethuvim*, meaning "writings." The Hebrew Bible is sometimes called *Tanakh* (or TNK), an acronym based on the three sections comprising the whole. Jesus himself attests to this threefold structure when he says, "Everything must be fulfilled that is written about me in the *Law of Moses, the Prophets and the Psalms*" (Luke 24:44).

The *Torah* section is considered the most important. It consists of the first five books of the Bible, commonly referred to also as the Books of Moses or the Pentateuch (from the Greek words, pente=five and teuchos=scroll). Tradition places Torah or Law in a class by itself because it embodies God's self-revelation to Israel, the chosen nation with which he made a covenant (agreement). Torah may be viewed as the core of three concentric circles. The Prophets and the Writings, represented by the outer circles, refer constantly to Torah and advocate its basic principles. Later we will examine how the Book of Psalms shares in this linkage to the Torah.

Psalms As Writings

The Psalter occupies a major seat in the *Kethuvim* or "Writings" division that has a total of eleven books.

In the diagram shown, Writings is represented by the outermost of three concentric circles. This section consists of very diverse genres of liter-ature. It ranges from the poetry of the Psalms to the royal accounts of Chronicles, to the heart-rending drama of Job.

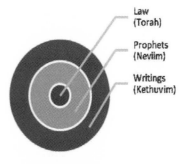

Organization of the Hebrew Bible

Psalms is represented in the Writings

Psalms is the longest in this section, making it representative of the whole. Luke 24:44 apparently reflects a tradition that placed Psalms at the head of the Writings, presumably because of its length.

Authorship

The headings present in most psalms indicate their authors.[9] Of the personal names prefixed to the psalms, the most common is David. About half of the entire Psalter is attributed to him. Solomon's name appears in the headings of Psalms 72 and 127. Psalm 90 is attributed to Moses. Other less familiar names include Asaph, Heman, Ethan and the sons of Korah. Authorship of the others cannot be determined.

On David

Because about half of the Psalms are associated with David, it has become Jewish custom to recognize David as author of the Psalter in the same way that Moses is to the Pentateuch (Genesis through Deuteronomy) and Solomon to wisdom literature (Proverbs through Song

Psalm Authors and their Works

Authors	Number of psalms	Psalms attributed according to titles
David	73	Psalms 3-9; 11-32; 34-41; 51-65; 68-70; 86; 101; 103; 108-110; 122; 124; 131; 133; 138-145
Asaph	12	Psalms 50; 73-83
Sons of Korah	11	Psalms 42; 44-49; 84-85; 87-88
Solomon	2	Psalms 72; 127
Moses	1	Psalm 90
Heman	1	Psalm 88
Ethan	1	Psalm 89
No author notated[10]	50	

of Songs).[11] We have more reason to take this tradition seriously when we read the New Testament, where six of the Psalms are particularly identified with David.[12]

As a composer, David embodied spirituality combined with musicality. His natural talent is well attested in the prophetic material of the Hebrew Bible.

- David wrote a song, recorded in 2 Samuel 22, as he celebrated God's deliverance.

- Earlier in his life, he came up with a dirge in 2 Samuel 1 as he lamented the deaths of Saul and Jonathan. (And he even required his people to learn it!) These compositions hold significant parallels to the Davidic psalms in tenor and style.

- David was also the one who instituted the ritual use of psalms in the presence of the Ark of the Covenant, the special wooden box which signified the Lord's presence (1 Chronicles 16:23–25).

Not surprisingly, at the end of David's life he acquires the title "Israel's singer of songs" (2 Samuel 23:1). Others render this as "The Sweet Psalmist of Israel."

On Asaph and the Korahites

A word should be mentioned about Asaph and the sons of Korah.

Asaph son of Barachias was one of the choir directors mentioned in 1 Chronicles 15:17. Apparently religious music ran in his blood, for in a later narrative, the "sons of Asaph" were chosen to prophesy "with harps and psalteries and cymbals" (1 Chronicles 25:1).

Asaphic psalms are skillful compositions with vivid imagery. They make for good teaching too, highlighting the providence of God throughout Israel's history. Perhaps the greatest honor given to Asaph is the placing of his name alongside that of David: "King Hezekiah and his officials ordered the Levites to praise the LORD with the words of David and of Asaph the seer" (2 Chronicles 29:30).

Eleven of the psalms are attributed to the Sons of Korah. As with Asaph, Korah's family hails from the tribe of Levi (2 Chronicles 20:19). They were assigned as temple singers but they were also composers.[13] Together, the Korahite songs promote a style that is unadorned yet elegant. Exuding the Levitical (or priestly) spirit, they underscore public worship, love for the Holy City, and unwavering trust in God.

Summary Points

- Psalms (Greek: *psalmoi*, Hebrew: *tehillim*) are lyric poems spoken by men to God, inviting us to experience how God's people in the past related to him.

- Jewish tradition universally located Psalms in the third section of the Hebrew Scriptures called "The Writings."

- Historically, the Book of Psalms is generally associated with Israel's monarchy, but dating each individual psalm is difficult.

- David wrote most of the psalms. Other authors are Moses, Asaph, Solomon, Heman, Ethan and the sons of Korah.

Getting Oriented

Books and Collections

Psalms is actually five books in one. Taking cue from Jewish usage, English Bibles show that the psalms are numbered and organized in five collections called "books." As will be shown later, the arrangement is topical, not chronological.[14]

Each book closes with a benediction or doxology (Grk: *doxazo* =to praise). The five benedictions mark off the five sections. Exactly how these books were compiled and ordered remains a mystery, but we do know that the compiler (possibly Ezra?) was very deliberate.[15] It is obvious that the five books in Psalms are to echo the five books of Moses or the *Torah*. This arrangement is akin to how

Five "Books" in One

Book 1 Psalms 1-41
Book 2 Psalms 42-72
Book 3 Psalms 73-89
Book 4 Psalms 90-106
Book 5 Psalms 107-150

Matthew (writing primarily to a Jewish audience) organized his Gospel around five discourses.

The Arrangement of the Book of Psalms[16]

Book Section	Number of Psalms	Has parallel themes in	Authorial attribution	Ending benediction
Book 1	41	Genesis	David – 37 Unknown – 4	41:13
Book 2	31	Exodus	David – 18 Korahites – 7 Asaph – 1 Solomon -1 Unknown – 4	72:19-20
Book 3	17	Leviticus	Asaph – 11 David -1 Korahites - 3 Heman – 1 Ethan -1	89:52
Book 4	17	Numbers	Moses – 1 David – 2 Unknown – 14	106:48
Book 5	44	Deuteronomy	David – 15 Solomon - 1 Unknown – 28	150 (whole psalm)

Within the Psalter are smaller, earlier collections. Most of these are designated by author. We have the Davidic collections (3-41, 51-70, 108-110, 138-145), the Asaphic Psalms (73-83), and the Korahite Psalms (44-49). Other groups follow themes. For instance, Psalms 93 through 100, with perhaps the exception of Psalm 94, are a compilation based on the common topic of God's kingship. This "album" is closed in thanksgiving by Psalm 100. Psalms 113-118 seem to be connected doxologies (praises). There is also a set called the Songs of Ascent (Psalms 120-134), which were likely sung as pilgrimage songs on the road to Jerusalem. Like Psalm 100, Psalm 134 serves as a fitting doxology to close this album.

A fairly complete listing of these collections is found in the Appendix of this book. Although the detailed history of its editorial working is not known, it is significant that the final form of the Psalter generally has a *topical* arrangement. Some comparisons can be easily drawn between the Psalter and hymnbooks of today. You will see in Chapters 4 and 10 that an awareness of the thematic linkages among psalms aids interpretation.

Psalm Titles

Majority of the psalms have titles or headings called superscriptions.[17] You will find a psalm's superscription inserted between the number of the psalm (say, "Psalm 3") and the first verse (Psalm 3:1). Most English translations include titles in the printed text of Psalms. This includes the NIV quoted most often in this book.

Psalm titles are very old. Dating at least two hundred years before the time of Christ, they were added primarily to aid understanding and guide liturgy or performance. There is not much we know about their origins, and they contain terms which remain puzzling. Some choose to dismiss them altogether. It would be wrong, however, to underestimate their value for study of the psalms.

Psalm titles offer valuable information and so are not to be ignored. Aside from indicating authorship, superscriptions may also specify the setting of a psalm. Some give musical references. Some offer direction for liturgy. A few give references to melodies that would have been known in the past.

Much ink has been spent on the study of titles. Scholars are divided on their authenticity. The question of when they were actually placed is also debated. I hold to the view that they are later additions to the text (i.e., I believe the psalms were not so titled at the moment they were composed), but nonetheless are inspired by God.[18]

Superscriptions are invariably included in Jewish textual tradition, where the psalm title is considered the *first verse* of the psalm. So, in the Hebrew, the title of Psalm 3 *is* Psalm 3:1. In contrast, many modern translations do not versify titles. This accounts for the difference in verse numbers between Hebrew Bibles and most English Bible.[19]

Information Provided by Psalm Titles

Information provided by title	Examples (in the NIV bible)
Author/s	Psalm 90, "A prayer of Moses the man of God." Ps 44, "Of the Sons of Korah."
Historical/occasional setting	Ps 3, "A psalm of David. When he fled from his son Absalom." Psalm 102, "A prayer of an afflicted man. When he is faint and pours out his lament before the LORD."
Musical character	Ps 45, "A *maskil*. A wedding song." Ps 60, "A *miktam* of David. For teaching."
Liturgical direction	Ps 4, "For the director of music. With stringed instruments." Ps 88, "A song. For the director of music. According to *mahalath leannoth*."

Psalms on David's Life

Of the information given in psalm headings, those pertaining to David are easiest to follow. There are seventy-three psalms which claim King David as their author.[20] Thirteen psalms have headings that refer to some event in his life (Psalms 3, 7, 18, 34, 51, 52, 54, 56, 57, 59, 60, 63 and 142), many of which are familiar to us. Some of these psalms relive the time of David's persecution under Saul, others his military triumphs. One refers to his sin with Bathsheba, another to his flight from Absalom.

Let's look at an example of a Davidic superscription, that of Psalm 34:

> Of David. When he pretended to be insane before Abimelech, who drove him away, and he left.

When this title was given or appended is unclear. What is clearer is the historical reference. The psalm heading seems to refer to the account in 1 Samuel 21:10-15. David feared for his life under King Achish of Gath (also called "Abimelech," a royal title rather than a personal name). David pretended to be crazy in hopes that the king would spare him and simply send him away. The contents of the psalm do fit well with the said account.

Using their titles, it is possible to align psalms with related events in David's life. Here is a partial list:

Psalm	Connected narrative in David's life	What the narrative tells us
59	1 Samuel 19:8-18	Saul, in a fit of jealousy, tries to kill David. By a thread he escapes, through no less than Saul's daughter Michal!
56, 34	1 Samuel 21:10-15	David, fearing for his life, pretends to be a madman. Achish was convinced and allows him to live. David praises God for his deliverance.
57	1 Samuel 24:1-22	In En Gedi, Saul is in hot pursuit of David. When Saul is caught in a compromised position, David could have killed him, but did not, proving that he was more merciful that Saul.
51	2 Samuel 12	David commits adultery with Bathsheba. He repents after a prophetic rebuke from Nathan.

To gain a greater understanding of the Davidic psalms, one good exercise is to read the narrative from David's life according to the historical books, followed by the related psalm. For instance, it is helpful to read 2 Samuel 12 which sets the backdrop for Psalm 51.[21] Reading the narrative behind it does much to illuminate this psalm, which is one of the most moving petitions one can find. The exercise also allows David's story to become yours. Do this for other psalms, and you will find that you can go beyond a surface acquaintance with David's compositions.

Types of Psalms

Psalms come in different types. The main ones are lament psalms, thanksgiving psalms, and praise psalms.

- Lament psalms are expressions of despair, usually accompanied by cries for help.

- Thanksgiving psalms give appreciation and credit for what God has done for the psalmist or for God's people.

- Praise psalms extol God for his character and qualities.

Several other types of psalms are to be found. Some psalms are called *wisdom psalms*. They teach and instruct us how to live and relate to God. Some psalms are *penitence* psalms, expressing self-examination or remorse. Some are songs of trust that articulate confidence and dependence on God and his care for us. The so-called *royal psalms* are about the anointed monarch through whom God's reign is established. *Enthronement psalms*, where Yahweh's reign is highlighted, may be seen as a subcategory of royal psalms. Others are combinations of different types. All these will be discussed thoroughly in Chapter 4.

But before we tackle individual psalms, it is necessary to discuss the fundamentals of reading the *poetry* of the Psalms. This vital topic occupies the upcoming chapter.

Summary Points

- Jewish tradition divides the Book of Psalms into five sections or "books." Within these five books, certain psalms have linkages or belong to smaller collections.

- Psalm titles should not be overlooked. Like road signs, they point you in the right direction.

- Psalms are of different types/categories. The three main categories are lament, thanksgiving, and praise.

Chapter Three

Psalms as Literature

Beautiful words fill my mind,
as I compose this song for the king.
Like the pen of a good writer
my tongue is ready with a poem.

—Psalm 45:1 GNB

EVER TRIED READING a newspaper in a foreign language? Unless you know the language, you won't get past the headlines!

For works written in unfamiliar languages, we rely on translations. Our Bibles render the Old and New Testaments from Hebrew and Greek respectively. So when we read a psalm in an English Bible, we are not reading the psalm as it was originally written; we are reading a translation.[22]

The psalms were originally written in ancient Hebrew, a language which has its own unique script and grammar. Psalms have certain features that are practically impossible to show using English translations. Examples include word play, word count, alliteration (sound repetition), acrostics, and acoustic rhythm (meter).

But we shouldn't despair. Fortunately for us, the most valuable things that can be learned about psalms do not require knowledge of Hebrew. They are surfaced in any language. (Though I must say that if you're actually thinking of learning Hebrew—that's not a bad idea! I don't regret my four semesters.) You will find that there are a good number of English translations available which adequately reproduce the original. Even so, to get into the Psalms, some important aspects of Hebrew prosody (poetic structure/composition) need to be studied.

Early Psalms

You probably know of some traditional songs in your own culture, melodies passed on through the generations. Each society has its own heritage of literary and musical arts. Much like their neighboring countries, the ancient Jews had a local culture which produced art in its various forms. Moreover, they were composing songs long before the time of the monarchy or the Temple, and different psalms were in circulation centuries before they were compiled.

It seems that the first psalms were written for individual occasions. Without organized religion, these early psalms were simply considered part of folklore. The ancients called them *shir* or *shirah*, meaning a song or a chant. Examples include Exodus 15:1-18 and Numbers 21:17-18. These compositions varied in subject matter, form and length. Interestingly, they exhibit characteristics similar to the songs in the Psalter and were included in the Old Testament as poetry. Peter Craigie gives us a list of these early psalms and poetic fragments:

Early Psalms and Poetic Fragments[23]

The Song of the Sea	Exodus 15:1-18
The Song of the Ark	Numbers 10:35-36
The Oracles of Balaam	Numbers 23-24
The Song of Moses	Deuteronomy 32
The Blessing of Moses	Deuteronomy 33
The Song of Deborah	Judges 5
The Song of Hannah	1 Samuel 2:1-10

You might want to study some of these early psalms and the narrative contexts (biblical stories) which produced them. This makes for great Bible study. For instance, you can read the story in Deuteronomy 31, which includes Moses' speech, and afterward read the related psalm in Deuteronomy 32, Moses' song. Similarly, you can read the historical account in Exodus 14 (Crossing of the Red Sea), then read the associated psalm in response to that event in Exodus 15 (Song of the Sea). Think of it as history enlarged by commentary—prose in Exodus 14 is amplified by poetry in Exodus 15.

Hebrew Poetry

Roses are red, violets are blue
Sugar is sweet, and you are *the same.*

> Twinkle, twinkle little star
> How I wonder what you are *made of*.

The above lines are well-known, but with a twist. You will notice that I changed some words. Now, I did not necessarily change the meaning (!), but the change is still "bothersome" because of how it sounds. The point is this: we expect poems to rhyme. Rhyme makes poems sound better and easier to remember.

Poetry of the Semitic (language family of Hebrew) kind differs from most Western poetry in that it does not rhyme the way we expect. Instead, we shall see, there is rhyming *of thought*. Such a feature makes the psalms different from other poems we know.

This brings us to the basics of Hebrew poetry. Two primary elements stand out: *parallelism* and *imagery*.

1. Parallelism

When Mary the virgin found out that she was to have a child, she sang a song, the *Magnificat*, which includes these beautiful lines:

> My being proclaims the greatness of the Lord,
> my spirit finds joy in God my savior. (Luke 1:46-47)

Exuberant Hebrew spirit takes artistic form here, showing the basic building block of Hebrew verse: short sentences that come in *pairs*. In Mary's song, we can easily see the correspondence between the two sentences. Verse 46 carries the same thought as verse 47. "My being" is parallel to "my spirit," and "proclaims" is parallel to "finds joy." The object of both verbs is essentially the same, "Lord" (v 46) and "God, my savior" (v 47).

The Terms

In Hebrew poems, the short sentence (a phrase in some cases) is called a colon. Two *cola* (plural of colon) combine to make what is technically called a *line*.[24] In the example above, Luke 1:46 is one colon, and it is paired with Luke 1:47, another colon. Together, Luke 1:46 and 47 make a poetic line. Occasionally three cola make a line, four cola in exceptional cases.

In most printed Bibles, the second colon of a line is slightly indented relative to the first. If a line has a third or fourth colon, these follow suit. Related lines are then combined in strophes (short stanzas) similar to Western poetry.

Note: A line does not necessarily constitute one verse; the two should not be confused. Luke 1:46-47 has assigned a verse number per colon, hence two verses in one line. But in Psalm 51:4, *two lines constitute one verse.*

> Line 1:   Against you, you only, have I sinned
>   and done what is evil in your sight,
> Line 2:   so that you are proved right when you speak
>   and justified when you judge. (Psalm 51:4)

As shown, the psalmists used the short sentence called the colon as their primary unit. In Hebrew poetry, the cola need not rhyme. Instead, there is rhyming of *thought*. Successive cola are paired (you could say "rhymed") to make a point or deliver an idea. This repeating or shadowing of clauses is called *parallelism*, a fundamental Hebrew literary device.

The Types

(If the following descriptions seem to get a bit on the technical side, I encourage you to make your way through it as it may very well bless you later on.)

Three basic types of parallelism can be seen in Psalms. *Synonymous parallelism* uses two (sometimes three or four) cola to express similar thoughts.

> The One enthroned in heaven laughs;
>   the LORD scoffs at them. (Psalm 2:4)

> Hasten, O God, to save me;
>   O LORD, come quickly to help me. (Psalm 70:1)

Pairs of cola can also be synonymous:

> The earth is the LORD's, and everything in it,
>   the world, and all who live in it;
> for he founded it upon the seas
>   and established it upon the waters. (Psalm 24:1-2)

> LORD, you have assigned me my portion and my cup;
>   you have made my lot secure.

> The boundary lines have fallen for me in pleasant places;
> surely I have a delightful inheritance. (Psalm 16:5-6)

Antithetic parallelism uses cola with contrasting thoughts:

> For the LORD watches over the way of the righteous,
> but the way of the wicked will perish. (Psalm 1:6)

> Calm your anger and forget your rage,
> do not fret, it only leads to evil. (Psalm 37:8)

When the second colon builds upon the thought of the first one, this is called *synthetic parallelism*.

> "I have installed my king
> on Zion, my holy hill." (Psalm 2:6)

> Ascribe to the LORD, O mighty ones,
> Ascribe to the LORD glory and strength. (Psalm 29:1)

In the above examples, the *synthesis* of the cola in Psalm 2:6 completes the thought (Zion) while in Psalm 29:1 it builds on the same word (the verb "ascribe").

One variation of synthetic parallelism[25] is called *emblematic parallelism* (one line explains the emblem in another):

> He makes me lie down in green pastures,
> he leads me beside quiet waters
> he restores my soul. (Psalm 23:2-3a)

Notice how the first and second clauses paint an image (making me lie down, leading me) and the last clause explains it (restoring).

In conclusion, you have seen that parallelism is a basic characteristic of Hebrew poetry. When reading the psalms, bear in mind that the thoughts generally come in pairs. Consider the parallel thoughts in order to grasp their meaning.

Excursus: Movement in Parallelism

We have already seen that Hebrew poetry uses short parallel sentences, usually in pairs. Aside from correspondence between cola, some scholars point out that there is also *movement* from the first colon to the second colon.[26] You could say there is some sort of addition. Let's look at two examples from Psalm 29.

> The voice of the LORD is powerful;
>   the voice of the LORD is majestic. (Psalm 29:4)

Note how both cola speak on the greatness of Yahweh's voice. Yet, there is a change in the adjective used, from "powerful" (Heb: *bakoach*) to "majestic" (Heb: *behadar*). The subsequent verse also shows movement, one of greater measure.

> The voice of the LORD breaks the cedars;
>   the LORD breaks in pieces the cedars of
>   Lebanon. (Psalm 29:5)

Like someone convincing his listeners by repeating and adding data, the writer goes from "cedars" to "cedars of Lebanon."[27] It's a lot like saying "...but not just any cedars, but those incredibly huge cedars, the ones you find in Lebanon."

Parallelism then, if we include the foregoing ideas, is *the art of saying something similar in both cola but with a difference added in the second colon*. This concept is vital for gaining insight. As Mark Futato remarks, "The Hebrew poets thus invite us to read slowly, looking for a difference in the second colon, be that difference small or great."[28]

So keep your eyes peeled for parallelism when reading the psalms. Read slowly, looking at how successive cola are placed in parallel. Try to discern the *difference* added from the first colon to next, and then see how the cola combine to deliver a more full thought.

2. Imagery

Word Pictures

Some time ago I received a text message on my cellphone. It read, "I am here." Attached to the message was a picture file. A friend of mine was on a hiking trip, and instead of describing in words the beauty of the place, he sent me a picture. That was all it took. A picture is worth a thousand words.

The second distinctive of Hebrew poetry is imagery — pictures to convey emotions and convictions. Inviting the reader to see with the mind's eye, the psalmists use *word pictures* on virtually every page.

They draw from ordinary, daily experiences, making it almost effort-less to go from reading the text to reflecting on it. Meaning and teach-ing are easily realized and accentuated by the illustrations drawn by words.

Examples

You don't have to go far into the Psalter to see the compelling use of pictures. Psalm 1 is loaded with imagery. There is the warning not to "sit in the seat of mockers." Those who make godly choices are lik-ened to a flourishing "tree," which is planted by "streams of water." In contrast, the ungodly are like useless "chaff" which the wind "drives away." The pictures lead the reader to the inevitable choice between blessedness and ruin (tree vs. chaff).

Within their rural culture, the psalmists drew their inspirations mostly from nature. From the most well-known Psalm 23, we have "The Lord is my Shepherd," "he leads me by still waters," and "makes me lie down in green pastures." In Psalm 19, David pictures God as a secure rock (19:14). In the same psalm, the steadfastness of God is proven by his promises, which are "more desirable than gold" and "sweeter also than honey and the drippings of the honeycomb" (19:10). Elsewhere, God's justice is like "the highest mountains" and his fairness like "the deepest sea" (36:6 NET). Appealing to dry Pales-tine, another psalm describes one's thirst for God in "a dry and weary land where there is no water" (63:1).

Inspiration from nature: Judean wilderness looking towards Moab

Psalm 104 ranks as one of the most image-filled poems. It speaks of life-giving water (104:10). It mentions wine and oil (104:15), referring to fertile vineyards and groves in the countryside. The mountains of Lebanon (104:18) do not escape notice. Animals are mentioned too—birds in verse 12 as well as goats and rabbits in verse 18.

Sample Imagery in Psalms

Purpose	Some of the images used
To depict God	shepherd, rock, fortress, king, guide
To depict God's people	sheep, inheritance, saints, throng, dove
To depict the psalmist's enemies	dogs, bulls, deceivers, lions
To depict God's word	lamp, honey, silver and gold

When reading psalms, pay attention to imagery. Think: the meaning is in the pictures. When we engage the word pictures in psalms, they engage us. As Leland Ryken points out, "Poetry is above all a very special use of language....Poetry is the language of images." He adds, "Readers of poetry need to think in images, just as poets do."[29]

Figures of Speech in Psalms

Skilled as they were, the psalmists had a variety of literary techniques at their disposal. Frequently and with great skill, they used figures of speech. By definition, a figure of speech occurs when a word or phrase is used in a sense other than the usual or literal sense. It is a departure from the everyday or typical use of words. In the Bible, figurative language makes for freshness, emphasis, and impact.

One common technique for building imagery in psalms is through *metaphor*. We are already familiar with metaphors such as "The Lord is my shepherd" and "Our God is a fortress." A metaphor is basically an association. It draws a correspondence between two things, often using word "is." When Psalm 84 declares that "The Lord God is a sun and shield," (v 11), it is not to be taken literally. God is likened to the sun and to a shield (a double metaphor) as one thinks about how protective he is to those he favors.

Personification (objects or concepts are given human qualities) is another favorite of the psalmists. This feature is found not just in

Psalms but in the Old Testament narratives as well (Genesis 4:7, "Sin is crouching at the door"). One of the best known examples of personification is in Psalm 23: "Your rod and your staff, they comfort me" (23:4). Here, the shepherd image is compounded by the rod and staff having a life of their own. They cannot comfort sheep by themselves. As tools, "rod" and "staff" (that is, their use by the shepherd) have the *effect* of comfort.

In their poems, the psalmists also described God by comparing him to humans and creatures. They used *anthropomorphism* (God is given human qualities) to communicate a proper view of God.

His eyes behold, his eyelids try, the sons of men. (Psalm 11:4)

Hide your face from my sins. (Psalm 51:9)

Zoomorphism is the term used for comparing God to animals. "I sing in the shadow of your wings," says Psalm 63:7b. Obviously, God in fact does not have wings. But his protection is such that we feel secure and sheltered.

Aside from comparisons with straightforward inter-pretation, substitutions are also common. Even without knowing the technical terms, we can detect them. In Psalm 22, the poet says, "Many bulls surround me" and "Dogs have surrounded me" (vv 12, 16). Are there real bulls and dogs here? The surrounding verses support the idea that the psalmist sees his enemies as bulls and dogs. Once you investigate the context, you have to return to the figure and ask why he compares them to such animals. Bulls and dogs attack. They are ferocious. The point is that the poet is in bad company and he feels powerless.

Another type of substitution is seen in Psalm 139:2: "You know when I sit down and when I rise." The psalmist writes this instead of saying God is aware of all his actions. It could also mean that God sees him the whole day. "Sit down" and "rise" serve as substitutes for other terms that could be used to bracket human activity. (The technical term is *merism*.)

Some other literary devices used are essentially substitutions: Often, the writer states the cause but intends the effect. A number of varieties exist. Sometimes psalmists substitute the cause for the effect or agent for product:

Their *throat* is an open grave. (Psalm 5:9)

Referring to the negative speech of the psalmist's enemies, the word used is throat (the agent of speech). In other cases, the effect is substituted for cause:

> Let me hear *joy and gladness*. (Psalm 51:8)

Instead of saying "Let me hear words of assurance," the poet places "joy and gladness," the *intended* effect of those words.

Synecdoche occurs when a part is substituted for the whole. In Psalm 23:5, David tells God, "You prepare a table before me..." There is no literal table meant here. The table stands for a richly prepared meal. So the NLT has "You prepare a feast for me..."

Finally there is *hyperbole*, purposeful exaggeration (or overstatement). A well-known example is found in the famous penitence psalm of David, Psalm 51. The backdrop of this psalm is a series of horrendous acts: David committed adultery with Bathsheba, abused his power, and orchestrated the murder of Uriah, one of his own men. But then, he says to God, "Against you, you only, have I sinned" (51:4). Surely he has offended others as well. This is not to say that he forgot how he has hurt people. He is speaking figuratively to express his intense guilt, grieving that his sin is so great that it "stinks to high heavens."

The same can be said about the next verse in Psalm 51, where David laments,

> Surely I was *sinful at birth*,
>   sinful from the time my mother conceived me. (Psalm 51:5)

"And in sin my mother conceived me," translates the NASB. Again, this points to the gravity of his sin. It is not saying that conception (or David's mother) is sinful, or that David sinned as a newborn. It is an exaggeration to reinforce the penitence in his heart. The expression leads to his urgent plea for restoration in the verses which follow (51:6ff).

To summarize, the psalms are literary works which frequently employ figurative language. Metaphor, personification, and various substitutions are used to convey their message.[30] The psalmists had "artistic license" and they used it.

Because figures of speech are not to be taken literally, readers should be careful in drawing meaning. We should not build dogma upon what may be figurative expressions. We should not expect systematic theology from the psalmists. What we *can* expect though, as we recognize these techniques, is a fuller understanding of the psalmists' situation, conviction, passion, and message.[31] This leads us to insights that will work their way into our hearts, and prayerfully, our lives.

Summary Points

- The psalms were originally written in the Hebrew language. Today we rely on translations when reading psalms.

- Early psalms and poetic fragments are found in the Old Testament. These were considered part of folklore.

- The two distinctive marks of Hebrew poetry are parallelism and imagery.

- The psalms use much figurative language and we should take note of interpretative rules.

Part Two

Into Their Message

God is more truly imagined than expressed, and he exists more truly than he is imagined.

— Augustine

To get the full flavor of an herb, it must be pressed between the fingers, so it is the same with the Scriptures; the more familiar they become, the more they reveal their hidden treasures and yield their indescribable riches.

— John Chrysostom

Chapter Four

The Types of Psalms

He has given me a new song to sing,
a hymn of praise to our God.
Many will see what he has done and be astounded.
They will put their trust in the LORD.

— Psalm 40:3 NLT

What Variety!

SONGS COME IN ALL SIZES AND SHAPES, much like the people who sing them. Our contemporary ears have been introduced to various songs aplenty—ballads, folk songs, nursery rhymes, jazz, rock-n-roll, rap. And then you have limitless combinations of those genres.

Now we don't listen to the national anthem the way we would listen to love songs. Similarly, we don't read a science fiction novel like a biography. Psalms come in rich variety and are to be "read" in different ways. *Understanding the types* of psalms guides our interpretation and facilitates understanding as well as application.

There is no standard way of classifying psalms; commentaries offer different ways. Early in the twentieth century, European scholars Hermann Gunkel and Sigmund Mowinckel made significant contributions to psalm study. Their main idea was to try to understand passages from Old Testament poetry by analyzing their literary structure.[32]

In his early work, Gunkel came up with five main types of psalms.[33] The chief criteria he used were

1. form or linguistic style, and
2. life setting (called *Sitz im Leben* in German) or worship setting.

Since Gunkel's proposal, details have been the subject of scholarly debates. Indeed, you can classify a psalm based on its form, style, theme/content, or how it was used in ritual. And no matter how you look at it, several psalms fit more than one category.

Form, Function, and Category

Despite the range of opinion on the types of psalms, there is a fairly common understanding on the importance of *form*.[34] Old Testament scholars who study poetic structures recognize that psalms of similar function take on some standard forms. These forms — keeping in mind that form and function are interrelated — largely determine *category*. [35] (Note that I use "type" and "category" interchangeably.)

Interestingly, there is a passage from the Chronicler explaining the purposes of liturgical music, suggesting as well how we might place the psalms in categories.

> They brought the ark of God and set it inside the tent that David had pitched for it, and they presented burnt offerings and fellowship offerings before God. After David had finished sacrificing the burnt offerings and fellowship offerings, he blessed the people in the name of the LORD....He appointed some of the Levites to minister before the ark of the LORD, to make petition, to give thanks, and to praise the LORD, the God of Israel. (1 Chronicles 16:1-4)

On that festive day, the Israelites brought the ark of God into a special tent and presented offerings. David, being the musician that he was, arranged for music to be played. Note how in the last sentence above (v 4), three *verbs* specify what the Levites were to do. Phrased in the Hebrew infinitive, the NIV does well to translate them, "to make petition, to give thanks, and to praise" the Lord. Correspondingly the ESV has, "to invoke, to thank, and to praise." This points us to the three major types of psalms: lament psalms (or petition psalms), thanksgiving psalms (or acknowledgement psalms), and praise psalms (or hymns).

Three Major Types of Psalms (based on 1 Chronicles 16:4)

Praise Psalms or Hymns	NIV: to praise	ESV: to praise
Lament or Petition Psalms	NIV: to make petition	ESV: to invoke
Thanksgiving or Acknowledgement Psalms	NIV: to give thanks	ESV: to thank

Major Types: Praise Psalms, Laments, Thanksgiving Psalms

Praise Psalms. Psalms of praise, also called *hymns,* extol God for his character and works. The popular expression "Hallelujah!" found in several psalms means "Praise God!" (*Hallel* means "praise," while "jah" or "yah" is short for "Yahweh.") Praise is acclamation. It refers to the action of ascribing to Yahweh what is due him. It is proper and fitting to praise God, says Psalm 147:1.

Praise psalms consist basically of four parts:

1. *Proclamation.* The psalmist initiates the tone of praise. He gives the intent of the psalm (to adore or give praise) and may invite others to do the same.

2. *Introductory Summary.* This part flows from the introduction and testifies about God's saving act/s.

3. *Report.* This part looks back to the time of need and describes deliverance from God.

4. *Conclusion.* This part praises God in a joyful manner. It may call others to join in worship.

It is possible to classify the praise psalms into four main types. Most common are *general hymns* (e.g., Psalms 67, 68, 103, 150) which praise God for a great variety of reasons, chiefly his majesty and perfect character. These may be rendered from the perspective of an individual or the community.[36] General hymns tell us to be exuberant; while there's a place for quiet appreciation of God, it is fitting to loudly exalt him. All are invited to the concert of celebration (117:1). The message is, "Let everything that has breath praise the Lord!" (150:6).

Other praise psalms may be called *creation hymns* (e.g., Psalms 8, 19, 33, 148). These songs marvel at God's creative power (8) or sovereignty over creation (33). They may invoke some reflection on the created realm itself (19, 65). The theme of Yahweh as King of the universe (29:10, 104:2ff) also finds expression in these psalms, as does the image of God as Provider-Sustainer (136:25, 104:10-18). Thus creation hymns invoke awe of God's greatness and likewise the gentleness of his care.

Some psalms praise God as Lord of History. These *salvation hymns* (e.g., Psalms 105, 106, 114, 135) are similar to epic poems. They contain narratives of God's mighty deeds throughout Israel's history. Much consideration is given to acts of deliverance, particularly the Exodus account when Israel was

Jerusalem is home to three religions: Christianity, Judaism, and Islam

delivered from bondage (105:12-25; 135:9). In these songs, God's nature leads him to intervene in history as he keeps his covenant of love (106:1, 135:3).

Songs of Zion (e.g., Psalms 46, 48, 87, 128) comprise the last subcategory of hymns. These psalms eulogize God's presence in the royal city, Zion or Jerusalem, and give praise to the city itself. The psalmists characteristically picture God making Zion his holy dwelling. The Lord "loves" the city, declares Psalm 87:2. Therefore the city and its inhabitants are secure against all threats. And because God is within the city ("in the midst of her"), it will "not be moved" (46:4-5 NASB).

Lament Psalms. Perhaps it should be of interest to us that lament psalms (sometimes called *petition psalms* or *complaint psalms*) are the most numerous. These psalms are primarily expressions of sorrow.

Their authors convey such feelings as abandonment, loss, and despair. They wrestle with issues such as suffering and injustice. The yield of troubled times, they are cries for deliverance, either from the individual (13, 22) or the community (74).

Do we wonder why so many psalms are laments? Like the rest of the Bible, the Book of Psalms reflects life as it is. Human experience is not always rosy; far from it! In the finely tuned realism of Hebrew poetry, lament passages explore the deep recesses of a person's pain. These verses can come across heavy. Yet it is there where valuable insights are gleaned. When trouble rains in torrents, we come to experience God in ways that we don't when all is going well.

The basic outline of the lament psalm features:

1. *Address/Invocation.* The psalmist has an introductory cry for help. He addresses God directly using various titles.

2. *Introductory Summary.* This lament portion introduces or summarizes the problem. It may also explain how difficult the situation is.

3. *Confession.* Following or interspersed within the next passage is a confession of trust. The psalmist expresses that his greatest hope is in God.

4. *Appeal.* This is a request for God to act favorably on behalf of the author. He uses words like "hear," "deliver," or "save."

5. *Reasoning.* The psalm may include some logic as to why God should intervene. It may further paint the hopelessness of the situation or "remind" God to protect his name or keep his promises. The psalmist might also reiterate his innocence, declaring that he has not turned to other gods for help.

6. *Conclusion.* This is an expression of hopeful expectations or thanksgiving that the prayer has been answered. It may also be a vow to proclaim in the future how faithful and reliable God is.[37]

Lament psalms tend to fall into five smaller categories. There are *general complaints* (e.g., Psalms 16, 28, 36, 77, 82), basically prayers of distress. In these psalms, the writers paint a broad picture of their plight without necessarily giving details. Although they are dominated by the language of petition (28), there are also assertions of trust in God (16). Also, the psalmists hold dearly to established spiritual truths in the midst of difficulty. Examples include the benefits of righteousness in contrast to wickedness (36:1-4) and reliance on God, without whom there is no hope (28:1).

Dominating the first two books of the Psalter are *prayers for deliverance.* Under this heading may be listed Psalms 3-5, 7, 25-27, 31, 69, 120, 139-143. In this subcategory, more effort is given to elaborate on the situation compared to general complaints (69). For instance, the psalmist might mention how he is being slandered and persecuted (31:13; 35:11, 15-16; 140:3) or falsely accused (7:1-2, 8; 35:19-21; 109:2-5, 25). In some cases there is an apparent threat to life (31:13; 69:4).

Some laments are *prayers for restoration of the community* (e.g., Psalms 14, 44, 53, 60, 74, 79, 126, 129, 137). These songs were markedly composed in the wake or in memory of some national disaster. Notable in these songs is great love for God's people (60), city (126), and temple (74). Their theology is anchored on God's loving relationship with his people, the Israelites, who are called by names of affection: "your dove" (74:19), "those you cherish" (83:3), "the sheep of your pasture" (74:1; 79:13).

Other laments (e.g., Psalms 6, 32, 38, 51, 143) may be called *psalms of penitence.* Also called *prayer songs of the sinner,* they are reflections on the divide between a perfect God and sinful man. The pangs of sorrow and guilt are articulated in great detail in these compositions (see especially Psalms 38 and 51). Here the psalmists reveal their inner thoughts in the wake of the tragedy of sin. They yearn for understanding and brokenness before God.

The final category of laments is *imprecatory psalms.* The designation is derived from Latin (*in/im*=toward; *precari*=pray). Also called cursing psalms, they "imprecate," wishing misfortune upon evildoers and invoking curses on enemies. They not only express despair and anguish, but on a "higher plane," look to God as the ultimate source of justice. Oftentimes, they also offer vivid suggestions on how God should fulfill justice. Because the practical theology of imprecatory passages can pose problems, an excursus or side discussion is provided (see Chapter 8).

Thanksgiving Psalms. These poems express thanks to God (as well as relief!) in response to some positive action or circumstance. Since they generally assume that God has acted already, they are also called *acknowledgement psalms.*

Thanks can be expressed in general terms (34) or for specific blessings such as recovery from serious illness (30). Some psalms express gratitude for forgiveness of sins (32, 103). Thanksgiving psalms can be written from an individual perspective (32, 34, 41, 103, and 138) or from a community perspective (65-68, 124).

Thanksgiving psalms typically have the following:

1. *Introduction.* It begins with a concise expression of praise or thanks (18:1-3; 30:1-3; 138:1-2).

2. *Call.* Attached to this introit might be a call for others to do the same (106:1-2).

3. *Summary Statement.* This line or couple of lines tells about what the Lord has done. Common words used are "deliver," "help," or "answer."

4. *Report.* The psalmist proceeds to expound on the account of healing or deliverance (18:6-19, 31-45; 32:5; 138:3ff). This portion is understandably the most lengthy.

5. *Conclusion.* The psalm ends with an expression of hopeful expectations or further thanksgiving.

Minor Types: Festival Songs, Royal Songs, Wisdom Songs

Psalm types other than praises, laments, and thanksgiving songs have been identified by scholars. Below are some categories which relate more to the *contents* of particular psalms rather than the form. As you sample them, it helps to know that poets would mix up different themes and elements in their composition. It would therefore be improper to treat these categories as mutually exclusive. And given the numerous elements shared among the psalm types, it is not surprising that scholars differ in their schemes of classification.

Festival Songs and Liturgical Psalms: 30, 50, 81, 115, 121, 122, 131, 134, 136. From one angle most of the psalms are liturgies of some kind, since they were generally composed for ritual use. However, certain psalms lay emphasis on public festivities or liturgical action. Significant portions of such psalms were obviously designed to accommodate certain elements of Jewish worship. The Sabbath day, for instance, saw the corporate recitation of Psalm 92. Psalm 81 relates to the New Moon festival. Psalms 113 and 118 (known as Hallel psalms) were sung on the night of the Passover,[38] and Psalm 30 was composed for the dedication of the temple site.

Royal Psalms: 2, 20, 21, 45, 47, 93, 96-99. This designation covers two types of psalms. In *royal psalms for the current monarch*, the subject matter is the incumbent king. The form can vary from petitions (20), to thanks (21), to odes on a royal marriage (45).[39] Other thematic links are found in Psalms 72, 101, and 110.

Certain royal psalms are called *enthronement psalms*. These poems visualize the kingship of the Lord and were probably part of an actual festival of enthronement.[40] Throughout the Ancient Near East, kingship was given high regard. In certain societies, the king was seen as a god or his physical representation. The psalms however emphasize the ultimate kingship of Yahweh. There is a repeated expression *malak yahweh*, roughly translated 'Yahweh is king' (46:8, 92:1, 95:3, 96:1).

Wisdom Psalms: 1, 34, 36, 37, 73, 105, 128. By their form and content these psalms share the characteristics of Old Testament wisdom literature (Job, Proverbs, Ecclesiastes).[41] Given they are designed to teach, they are also called *didactic psalms* (*didactic*=meant for instruction). In the Ancient Near East, teachers of wisdom were concerned with order and justice (or righteousness) in the created world. It is probable that wisdom psalms originated as proverb-like verses which were used by Hebrew teachers for instruction.

Often of a more tranquil mood, wisdom psalms extoll the merits of the wise life. *Hokmah* (Hebrew for "wisdom") refers to not just intellectual capacity. Wisdom is concerned with the application of truth to practical living. Wisdom passages may offer an image of the ideal (133) or contrast pictures of good and bad choices (1, 37). In addition, they caution against ungodly attitudes. Overall, they associate godliness with good choices.

Now that we've gone through all the basic types, we can tabulate the psalms according to category:

The 150 Psalms Categorized

Psalm Type	The Psalms
Praise Psalm – General Hymn	67-68, 75, 103, 113, 115, 117, 134, 146-147, 149-150
Praise Psalm – Creation Hymn	8, 19, 29, 33, 65, 100, 104, 136, 148
Praise Psalm – Salvation Hymn	47, 78, 105, 106, 114, 135, 136
Praise Psalm – Song of Zion	46, 48, 76, 84, 87, 122

Lament Psalm – General Complaint	16, 28, 36, 77, 82, 123, 125
Lament Psalm – Prayer for Deliverance	3-5, 7, 9-13, 17, 26-27, 31, 35, 42-43, 54-59, 62-64, 69-71, 86, 94, 109, 120, 139-143
Lament Psalm – Prayer for Restoration	14, 44, 53, 60, 74, 79, 80, 83, 85, 90, 108, 126, 129, 137
Lament Psalm – Psalm of Penitence	6, 25, 38-41, 51, 88, 102, 130
Lament Psalm – Imprecatory Psalm	5, 10, 17, 35, 58-59, 69-70, 79, 83, 109, 129, 137, 140
Thanksgiving Psalm	18, 22-23, 30, 32, 34, 40, 52, 66, 92, 107, 116, 118, 124, 138
Festival Songs and Liturgical Psalms	30, 50, 81, 115, 121-122, 131, 133
Royal Psalm – Current Monarch	2, 20, 21, 45, 61, 72, 89, 101, 110, 132, 144
Royal Psalm–Enthronement of Yahweh	2, 24, 47, 93, 95-99, 145
Wisdom Psalm	1, 15, 19, 34, 37, 49, 73, 78, 91, 111-112, 119, 127-128

Psalms with Special Features

I have already mentioned that some psalms will not be simply confined to one location. Cutting across the different types, we find certain psalms with special features.

Acrostic Poems: 9, 10, 25, 34, 37, 111, 112, 119, 145. Some psalms are so written that the initial letters of consecutive lines form an alphabet, word, or phrase. In Psalms 111-112 for instance, each line begins with an in-sequence Hebrew letter. In Psalm 119, eight lines are devoted to each letter of the Hebrew alphabet. Parallels exist in other Old Testament books, particularly those with poetic elements (Proverbs 31:10-31, Nahum 1:2-20, Lamentations). Acrostics were used as mnemonic tools (memory devices), conveying ideas of order, progression, and completeness.

Messianic Psalms: 2, 8, 16, 22, 41, 45, 69, 72, 89, 102, 109-110, 118, 132. As a whole, the psalms carry a yearning for a time when God's rule will be felt throughout the world. The focus of this aspiration is the coming Messiah (see Chapter 7). Messianic psalms predict or depict the coming of the messiah in the person of Jesus Christ. Different aspects of the life of Christ are touched upon. Christ himself explains that the psalms speak about him (Luke 24:44).

Pilgrimage Psalms (Songs of Ascent): 120-134. These fifteen psalms are also called *Songs of Degrees.* Scholars have advanced various theories on the significance of these songs. They were probably sung on the journey to Jerusalem or as people approached the Temple.[42] In these psalms, there seems to be a progression of thought. The series echoes the Psalter's extensive movement from distress (120) to praise (134), ending on a faithful and confident note.

Psalms of Intercession: 20, 67, 112, 122, 132, 134, 144. These psalms, mostly of the lament type, ask God to move on behalf of Israel. Here the psalmists paint a picture of grave need, begging Yahweh to deliver his people, or implore him for blessing.[43]

Songs of Confidence: 4, 11, 23, 61, 62, 91, 129. Also called *Songs of Trust,* these poems emphasize assurance and trust in God. They affirm God's faithful-ness. A prime example is Psalm 23. Others similarly express secu-rity and assurance in God. When trouble is all around, we can either panic or find strength in faith. In these psalms the writer sees God as his ultimate Protector. Like the laments, songs of trust can be individual (4, 11, 23, 121) or communal (115, 125, 129).

Table of Dominant Psalm Types per Book

Book or collection	Psalms included	Dominant types	Some other types included
Book 1	1-41	Laments mostly	Messianic—22 Song of Trust – 23 Acrostic Psalm– 37
Book 2	42-72	Laments mostly	Royal Psalm – 45 Thanksgiving – 65-68 Messianic – 69
Book 3	73-89	Laments mostly	Wisdom Psalm – 73 Historical Psalm – 78 Messianic – 89
Book 4	90-106	Praise mostly	Song of Trust—91 Royal Psalm—93 Historical Psalm—105-106
Book 5	107-150	Praise mostly	Thanksgiving Psalm—107 Royal Psalm—110 Creation Psalm—148

Summary Points

- The three main types of psalms are laments, praise psalms, and thanksgiving psalms. A majority of the psalms contain some kind of lament.
- Some other types of psalms based on content are festival (and liturgical) psalms, royal psalms, and wisdom psalms.

Questions for Study and Discussion

1. Consider that psalms are like "living snapshots." In what ways do the various types of psalms mirror a person's life?

2. How can your life reflect the infectious enthusiasm of the praise psalms?

3. Why is "wisdom" more than just "being smart"?

4. How are messianic psalms relevant for us today?

Chapter Five

The God of the Psalmist

Who is so great a God as our God?

—Psalm 77:13b

I REMEMBER TRYING TO WRITE a valentine card for my girlfriend some years ago.

Now to be honest I'm not the romantic type—I'm more of the stiff, quirky, science-and-history guy. I'm not an artist, certainly not a poet. But somehow or other, I managed. Surprisingly, the words seemed to flow. It was like lines emanated from some deep mystical source. And I think I did an okay job. (My girlfriend, Weng, is now my wife!)

But before you think I'm getting mushy, let me get my point across: *relationships naturally inspire creative expression*. If you've ever been in love, you know what I mean. In the case of the psalmists, their relationship with God resulted in original poetry. They thought about God. They spoke to him and about him.

The psalms are products of the poets' contemplations. They spring from inspired thought. As S.R. Driver explains:

> The Psalms…consist of reflections, cast into a poetical form, upon the various aspects in which God manifests Himself either in nature, or towards Israel, or the individual soul.[44]

So the main motivation for writing psalms is God himself. God is the source as well as the object of inspiration. He is the beginning and the end of creative composition. And before they were devoted to their craft, the poets were, above all, devoted to God.

Picturing God

The God of the psalmists was very real to them. The images used to depict God demonstrate this. He is never described as some distant concept, never rendered as some lifeless force. The favorite picture of God is anthropomorphic — portraying him as if he were a person. God is given a mouth, nostrils, and ears. He ponders, laughs, shouts, gets angry, spreads a table, brandishes a sword, and shoots arrows. The lush images leave imprints in our minds.

- God is portrayed as a father who loves and cares.
- He is seated in glory like a king and causes the heavens to bow.
- He is a mighty warrior who scatters the enemies of his people.
- He is a shepherd who tends his sheep with protective compassion.

The presentation of God as a person brings him close to us as readers. The psalms invite us to consider how great a God he truly is.

Who is this great God whom the psalmists sang and prayed to? Let us encounter him through the psalms.

One God

The psalmists recognized their God as the one true God. No credence is given to other deities; no apologies made. Even in passages which talk about other "gods" (e.g., 96:4, 97:9), there is no debate on the matter. The other gods are *nothing*.

> For who is God besides the LORD?
> And who is the Rock except our God? (Psalm 18:31, Psalm 35:10a)

> For who in the skies above can compare with the LORD?
> Who is like the LORD among the heavenly beings? (Psalm 89:6)

> The Mighty One, God, the LORD,
> speaks and summons the earth from the rising of the sun to the place where it sets. (Psalm 50:1)

This one God, the psalms insist, is the Creator and Designer of the universe (8:3). He is both Source and Sustainer of all things (19:1-6), the Maker and Preserver of man (139:14, 36:6).

The First Commandment

There is a solid base for monotheism (*mono*=single; *theos*=God) in the psalms. Although the individual psalms were written in a span of many centuries, there is no doubt that they are all anchored on the earlier teaching found in the Torah. At Mount Sinai, where Yahweh contracted his covenant (relational agreement) with the Israelites, he gave them the Decalogue or Ten Commandments (Exodus 19-20). It was a pivotal time for Israel because these basic commandments embodied divine principles. They outlined what it means to be a people who follow Yahweh. In other words, it was a constitution.

To become God's people, Israel was to adhere to some basic tenets. God began with the stipulation of monotheism. The first commandment boomed: Have no god apart from Yahweh.

> "I am the LORD your God, who brought you out of Egypt, out of the land of slavery. You shall have no other gods before me." (Exodus 20:2-3)

God laid this as the footing on which other teachings were built. The Ten Commandments rest squarely on the premise that God is the only God who deserves recognition.

So important was this basic truth that it was revisited before they entered the Promised Land (Deuteronomy 5-6).

> "I am the LORD your God, who brought you out of Egypt, out of the land of slavery. You shall have no other gods before me." (Deuteronomy 5:6-7)

> Fear the LORD your God, serve him only and take your oaths in his name. (Deuteronomy 6:13)

No Idols

Additionally, and as a direct consequence of the First Commandment, Israel was not to make any idols ("any graven image" in the KJV, Deuteronomy 5:8ff). This was Commandment Two. Yahweh was not to be contained or misrepresented. When we fast forward several centuries later to the time of the monarchy and the

Temple, we find the no-images teaching still in force. In keeping with strict monotheism, no idol was to be found in Israel's Temple. When the psalms were used in worship, they underscored the idea that no *physical* representation of God could be substituted for him.[45] Only *literary* images were used to illustrate the one God of the psalmists. To these images we now turn our attention.

God As King

There is one divine image that stands out in the Book of Psalms: God is a reigning king. The second psalm, one of the most quoted in the New Testament, sets off the kingship theme like a banner.

> The One enthroned in heaven laughs;
> > the LORD scoffs at them.
> Then he rebukes them in his anger
> > and terrifies them in his wrath, saying,
> "I have installed my King
> > on Zion, my holy hill." (Psalm 2:4-6)

> Therefore, you kings, be wise;
> > be warned, you rulers of the earth.
> Serve the LORD with fear
> > and rejoice with trembling.
> Kiss the Son, lest he be angry
> > and you be destroyed in your way,
> > for his wrath can flare up in a moment.
> Blessed are all who take refuge in him. (Psalm 2:10-12)

Although the text begins speaking of kings on earth (vv 1-3), the scene immediately shifts to heaven from where God rules. He is "the One enthroned" there (v 4).

Earlier I talked about a category of psalms called *enthronement psalms* (e.g. Psalms 2, 24, 47, 93, 95-99, 145). Characteristic of this group is the tribute given to Yahweh as king. Psalm Two is a leading sample. The poet imagines Yahweh upon the throne to wield his royal power. His presence invokes awe and respect.

But the picture of God as king is not found only in the enthronement psalms. Throughout, many psalms promote this monarchical picture of God through titles of kingship. Here is a list of related titles:

Kingship Titles for God in Psalms

"King" (5:2; 10:16; 29:10: 44:4; 47:6; 84:3; 89:18; 98:6; 145:1; 149:2)
"Great King" (48:2)
"A great King over all the earth" (47:2, 7)
"A great King above all gods" (95:3)
"The King of glory" (24:7-10)
"My King" (68:24)
"My King of old" (74:12)

God is designated King in each of the five books of the Psalter, about twenty times in sum. The poets repeatedly use statements like "The Lord is King" (six times) and "The Lord reigns" (seven times). In Book 4, particularly in the grouping of Psalms 93-99, Yahweh's sovereign rule comes to expression frequently:

> The LORD is king! (Psalm 93:1 NLT)

> For the LORD is the great God, the great King above all gods. (Psalm 95:3 NLT)

> Say among the nations, "The LORD is king!" (Psalm 96:10a NRSV)

> Make a joyful symphony before the LORD, the King! (Psalm 98:6 NLT)

The idea projected is that Yahweh is not just King over Israel; he is sovereign over all the nations. He is supreme royalty, swaying his scepter over all. Having established his realm in various spheres, it is proper that all worship him, even those beyond Israel's borders.

Throughout Psalms, expressions of praise are expanded and modified by the theme of God as king. I see it as mindset. It is easy to imagine that the Israelites carried God's kingship in their consciousness as they worshipped, and the psalmists led the way. Indeed, the Book of Psalms is about the Kingdom of God.[46]

God's Reign of Power

How does one begin to describe God's reign? For the psalmists, two things stand out as God works through the office of King: power

and protection. Let us discuss power first. A king would not be king
if he did not have power. The psalmists show that God is inherently
powerful (89:13, 147:5). He is like a king in his palace wielding carte
blanche (66:7, 63:2, 68:34). His power cannot be hidden or taken for
granted (77:14, 66:3, 106:8).

The psalmists describe God as an unrivalled ruler who subdues
nations. Not to be taken lightly or casually, he is a potentate to be
feared and revered. So Psalm 66 states:

> Say to God, "How awesome are your deeds!
> So great is your power
>> that your enemies cringe before you. (Psalm 66:3)

> He rules forever by his power,
>> his eyes watch the nations —
>> let not the rebellious rise up against him. *Selah* (Psalm 66:7)

The psalms use several titles and images to describe God's power.
One common motif is that of *strength*. The word "horn" (Heb: *qeren*),
suggesting a battling animal, is used figuratively in the Old Testament
to denote aggressive strength (Daniel 8:7, 1 Kings 22:11).[47] No doubt,
David had this in his mind in Psalm 18, where he proclaims the Lord
as "the horn of my salvation" (v 2). David is acknowledging the power
of God over him, how that power works on his behalf. The same idea
is found in Psalm 89:17, where the words "horn" and "strength" are
used in parallel to describe God strengthening his people. God is the
"glory of their strength." That is, God is so strong that he is able to
give strength to those in his favor.[48] Psalm 68:35 sums it well and adds
a note of praise:

> You are awesome, O God, in your sanctuary;
>> the God of Israel gives power and strength to his people.
> Praise be to God! (Psalm 68:35)

Here are some authoritative titles used for God in psalms:

- The Most High (used 18 times)[49]
- The Highest (18:13)
- Greatly exalted (47:9)
- The mighty God (50:1)
- My strong tower (61:3 NRSV)

- My tower of safety (144:2 NLT)
- My glory (62:7 KJV)
- The judge (75:7)
- The high God (78:35)
- The Holy One of Israel (78:41, 89:18)

One title that deserves mention is "God of hosts" (80:7, 14 KJV). The word "hosts" in the Hebrew context refers to a mass of people, that is, an army. The image conjured is a great campaign. Eighteen times in Psalms (KJV), God is cast in the role of a commanding officer. His inherent power convinces one to take courage and confidence. So the Korahites declare, "O LORD of hosts," "Blessed is the one who trusts in you!" (84:12).

God's Reign of Protection

The power of God does not make him distant or aloof or abusive. In contrast to typical earthly powers, God is not a tyrant. God is not like us; he is not prone to human corruption when exerting authority. The psalms maintain that God, despite his power, is not closed off from his people. He connects. He listens when they speak to him, and he responds to their prayers.

The psalms report to their hearers that God uses his power to protect.

"Because of the oppression of the weak
    and the groaning of the needy,
I will now arise," says the LORD.
    "I will protect them from those who malign them."
(Psalm 12:5)

You are my hiding place;
    you will protect me from trouble
    and surround me with songs of deliverance. (Psalm 32:7)

"Because he loves me," says the LORD, "I will rescue him;
I will protect him, for he acknowledges my name. (Psalm 91:14)

Yahweh is a paragon of protective compassion. Like a constant guardian, he watches over his people with care.

No doubt the most popular image of protection is found in Psalm 23:1, "The Lord is my shepherd." Psalm 80:1 falls in, calling Yahweh the "Shepherd of Israel." Other key motifs abound. God is metaphorically called "shield" in eight of the psalms, and in one case, "a sun and a shield" (84:11). Some call him "strong tower" (61:3), "fortress" (28:8), and "my strong habitation" (71:3 KJV). To others he is "keeper" (121:5) and "deliverer" (144:2).

The psalmists also avail of some more tender images and titles to describe God's protective hand:

- As a bird protecting her young (61:4)
- My God, in whom I trust (91:2 NASB)
- The God of my mercy (59:10, 17 KJV)
- Shade upon your right hand (121:5)
- An ever-present help in trouble (46:1)
- Helper of the fatherless (10:14)

Some images and titles are recurrent, suggesting a strong biblical theme.[50] One of these, the *refuge metaphor,* will be developed in a later section.

Images of Power and Protection

We have seen that God's reign includes aspects of power and protection. The psalmists were convinced that these two facets sync well in the God whom they worshipped. We now consider some illustrations.

Father

Among the testimonies for God in Psalms, one uses a filial image—God as a father:

A father to the fatherless, a defender of widows,
is God in his holy dwelling. (Psalm 68:5)

As a father has compassion on his children,
so the LORD has compassion on those who fear him
(Psalm 103:13)

Psalm 68 locates Father God in his "holy dwelling," from where he watches over those who are defenseless—orphans and widows. In Psalm 103, God safeguards people with compassion. Despite much reason to fear him, he shows compassion as a father.

The above verses affirm a well-known fact, one that we know from real life: fatherhood entails *both* power and protection. (Would you dads agree?) I am in a position of authority in my family. Given that my wife and kids recognize this, they have a natural expectation that I would protect them. This I would do, with my own life if necessary. My being a father makes me focus my power *towards protecting those I love*. Reflecting on this fact helps me appreciate God as a powerful, protective father.

Rock

From the father image we now turn to the image of a rock. Rejoicing after a victory, David declares, "The LORD is my rock" (Psalm 18:2). The word "rock" (Heb: *sela*) can mean "stone" or "rock formation." It denotes stability and defense, a powerful illustration of God's power and protection. Other titles expand the metaphor:

- My Rock (18:46, 19:14, 28:1, 31:3, 42:9, 62:2, 71:3)
- My strong rock (31:2)
- The rock of my strength (62:7 KJV)
- The rock of my salvation (89:26)
- The rock of my refuge (94:22)
- The Rock that is higher than I (61:2)
- Rock of our salvation (95:1)

King

Going back to our earlier metaphor, the psalms carry the theme of God as a powerful king who watches over his kingdom and lovingly saves his subjects from adversity. Hinged upon the account of the Exodus (e.g., 68:7-10), their theology is consistent with the history of God's people. Yahweh forged a covenant relationship with Israel. He has made himself to be Master and Protector to his covenant people. He can be counted on to do this, not only because he has the might, but because he cares (power and protection). Psalm 62 captures both facets of God's reign:

> One thing God has spoken,
> two things have I heard:
> that you, O God, are strong,
> and that you, O LORD, are loving.
> Surely you will reward each person
> according to what he has done. (Psalm 62:11-12)

God is strong *and* loving. Power and love are not mutually exclusive, especially in God. In fact, God's advocacy is made certain by his authority. Notice how the two aspects are fused by David in Psalm 18, where God is pictured as a reliable and vigorous defender:

> He reached down from on high and took hold of me;
>   he drew me out of deep waters.
> He rescued me from my powerful enemy,
>   from my foes, who were too strong for me.
> They confronted me in the day of my disaster,
>   but the LORD was my support. (Psalm 18:16-18)

David understood that a great champion had come to his rescue. Although the enemy forces were strong, the Lord prevailed over them.

As king, God uses his power not for his own ends, but for the benefit of his people. He is savior and protector. He judges (rules) with integrity. When he gets angry, it is not out of whim. His indignation compels him to vindicate the righteous. The psalms tell and retell such stories of deliverance. All these stem from God's perfection, in which positive virtues are balanced and harmonized.

Summary Points

- The psalms assume a strict monotheism: There is no God but the Lord (*Yahweh*).
- The psalmists portray God as a great king. Their writings abound in images of power and protection.

The Temple: God's House

When people invite you to their house, it means something. It's a privilege. You're a guest. When God invites you to *his* house, it means something. You are privileged, an honored guest. The psalmists were invited to God's house. They rejoiced and sang about it.

Significance

Because the psalms are about God, *where* God dwells is considered highly important. During the time of the monarchy, the Temple was seen as God's house. David had conceived it to be that way. Just as David had a palace from which to rule, so did God (2 Samuel 7:5-7).

As the abode of God, the Temple was to reflect his glory. People were to come to it with reverence. It was to be a sanctuary, a holy place of prayer and worship.[51] Just like the Tabernacle (special worship tent)[52] before it, the Temple was to symbolize and denote God's presence.

As plans were made for the building of the Temple, David set up the orders of singers and musicians which should be responsible for the praise of God in the sanctuary (1 Chronicles 25). He also composed many of the psalms that were eventually sung during worship.[53] Community worship was built up and singing highlighted. Thus the Temple became the subject of many psalms.

> In my distress I called to the LORD;
> I cried to my God for help.
> From *his temple* he heard my voice;
> my cry came before him, into his ears. (Psalm 18:6)

> One thing I ask of the LORD, this is what I seek:
> that I may dwell in the house of the LORD
> all the days of my life,
> to gaze upon the beauty of the LORD
> and to seek him in *his temple*. (Psalm 27:4)

> Within *your temple*, O God,
> we meditate on your unfailing love. (Psalm 48:9)

Other passages may not directly say "temple" (Heb: *hekal*) but refer to it as God's abode. We are familiar with Psalm 23 expressing confidence to stay forever in the "house of the Lord" (also in 122:9).

- When speaking *to* God, the psalmists refer to the Temple as "Your house" (84:4, 93:5).
- Psalm 42:4 refers to a procession to the "house of God" (also in 55:14).
- Psalm 26:8 has, "the house where you live, O LORD."
- Psalm 43:3 has, "the place where you dwell."
- Others psalms say "dwelling" (74:7, 132:7).

Temple-ward Thoughts

Whatever it was called, the Temple was always associated with pleasant things. The Temple was a safe haven, intimately connected with God himself. It signified strength, hope, and growth.

But I am like an olive tree
    flourishing in the house of God. (Psalm 52:8a)

Blessed are those you choose
    and bring near to live in *your courts!*
We are filled with the good things of *your house,*
    of *your holy temple.* (Psalm 65:4)

Among the psalms, one that perhaps reflects the greatest yearning for God's house would be Psalm 84. It is a Song of Zion (Jerusalem)[54], written or edited by the Sons of Korah. The text brims with enthusiasm to be in God's house. Pondering on these verses, the excitement is palpable.

How lovely is your dwelling place,
    O LORD Almighty!
My soul yearns, even faints, for the courts of the LORD;
    my heart and my flesh cry out for the living God.
(Psalm 84:1-2)

Blessed are those who dwell in your house;
    they are ever praising you. (Psalm 84:4)

Better is one day in your courts
    than a thousand elsewhere;
I would rather be a doorkeeper in the house of my God
    than dwell in the tents of the wicked. (Psalm 84:10)

Relevance

What could this emphasis on the Temple mean for us today? Does it hold any relevance at all? Certainly. As an image (again, the staple of Hebrew poetry), the Temple is one of many biblical pictures that show a progression. It is part of an unfolding story about God's *abiding presence* that concludes with us.

Even a cursory look at this progression reveals something about God: He desires to be fellowshipped and experienced. God first created the heavens and the earth as a backdrop for humanity (Genesis 1). He made his presence known at the Garden of Eden (Genesis 3). Later on, God rescued his people the Israelites and guided them through a Pillar of Cloud (Exodus 13-14). Then God commanded Moses to build the Ark of the Covenant (Exodus 25). The Ark represented God's presence (1 Samuel 5). Going further, God would dwell in his Tabernacle (Numbers 11), then the Temple (1 Kings 8).[55] After that, through the Incarnation, God took on flesh in Jesus (John 1) in order to dwell with men.

After Jesus' ascension, the next and final step was to send the Holy Spirit (John 16). God himself was to dwell, not around us, but *inside* us. The Apostle Paul says that we as Christians are now *the* Temple of the Living God:

> Don't you know that you yourselves are God's temple and that God's Spirit lives in you?...God's temple is sacred, and you are that temple.
> (1 Corinthians 3:16-17)

> ...For we are the temple of the living God. As God has said: "I will live with them and walk among them, and I will be their God, and they will be my people." (2 Corinthians 6:16)

Paul in fact extends the metaphor by saying that the church of disciples is like a holy temple: "In him the whole building is joined together and rises to become a holy temple in the Lord" (Ephesians 2:21).

Do you see the biblical story being unfurled? God dwelling in the universe… God dwelling in a Garden… God dwelling in a box (the Ark)… God dwelling in a tent (the Tabernacle)… God dwelling in a building (the Temple)… God dwelling in Jesus… God dwelling in *us!*

All these show that God has eagerly desired to be with people. He has been that way ever since, constant through the ages. He wants to fellowship. He envisions community.

No wonder the psalmists so longed for the Temple. It was not just a building. Being there was not about some ritual. It was about being with God, the God who desires solidarity with his people. Even the psalmists' greatest desires for the Temple were eclipsed by the desire of the One in the Temple. In writing their masterpieces, the Hebrew poets knew this: All they were doing was reflecting back to God the passion for fellowship that they found in him.

Summary Points

- The Book of Psalms has been called the songbook of the Temple.

- As the hub of Israel's worship during the Monarchy, The Temple became the subject of many psalms.

- The Temple motif emphasizes the unfolding story of God's desire to have a people for himself and to fellowship with them.

Questions for Study and Discussion

1. The psalmists were fully devoted to their God, the one true Go. Nowadays, what are some "gods" that people devote their lives to?

2. How has God shown his power and protection to you?

3. Why is the "father" metaphor important for Christian living?

4. How does the Temple reflect God's desire for community?

Chapter Six

Extensive Themes in Psalms

Your decrees are the theme of my song wherever I lodge.

—Psalm 119:54

YOU CAN TELL A LOT about a person by looking through his or her photo collection—snapshots, whether placed in a traditional album, stored in an electronic device, or hung on the wall. Similarly, the Psalter "introduces" itself as a collage of pictures.

Psalms are living snapshots, and "looking through" them we gather what the whole Psalter is all about. We take in messages and ideas. We unravel a story. The psalms might appear disconnected and random, but themes weave throughout and tie things together.

God is the center-of-gravity of these themes. All thematic elements are firmly based on God's steadfast character and timeless principles. Articulated adeptly and cogently, they are frequently reinforced, at times jumping at you with such force, elsewhere gently fading in.

Allow me to present four, extensive, Bible-wide themes from the Book of Psalms: Happiness, Choices, Hope, and The Coming Messiah. The first three will be tackled in this chapter, the fourth under the heading of "Jesus in the Psalms" in the next.

1. Happiness

Everybody wants to be happy. So go lines from rock stars and philosophers. Look around and you will see people pursuing happiness (however they might define it). In the best-selling book

Happiness, the immensely popular Harvard professor Tal Ben-Shahar calls happiness "the ultimate currency." Somehow, people recognize happiness as a standard by which to assess worth and make decisions.

The Book of Psalms is about happiness, *true* happiness. This we discover from its opening. If you want to know what a book is about, the best place to look is in the introduction. Psalms 1 and 2 form a prologue like two framing doorposts. They usher you into the book. Taking your first steps inside, you are met by the word "blessed," meaning "happy."

> Blessed ["happy" NRSV, NAB] is the man
>> who does not walk in the counsel of the wicked
> or stand in the way of sinners
>> or sit in the seat of mockers.
> but his delight is in the law of the LORD,
>> and on his law he meditates day and night. (Psalm 1:1-2)

Notice the first word in Psalms is the word "blessed" (Heb: *ashrey*). This Hebrew word is pregnant with meaning. "Blessed" does mean happy, but is more than a feeling. The opening line could be translated, "Truly happy is the man who…" or "The happiness of the man who…" The NLT has, "Oh, the joys…" while the NET Bible prefers "How blessed…" Evidently, one translation is not enough to get the nuances across. *Ashrey* is dense; it goes beyond the emotional realm.

The Meaning

Blessedness is about confidence and providence. It is a special (even enviable) condition which is associated with God's favor.[56] This definition is supported by the image of the flourishing tree in verse 3 of the same psalm:

> He is like a tree planted by streams of water,
>> which yields its fruit in season
>> and whose leaf does not wither.
> Whatever he does prospers. (Psalm 1:3)

The living tree image[57] of Psalm 1 illustrates the happiness of the man who is prospered by God. "Tree" is rendered in contrast to "chaff," a metaphor for the wicked (1:4). Building on those analogies, Psalm 2 shows the futility of going against God. World powers may be in uproar against God's anointed, but this amounts to nothing. God merely derides and rebukes them (2:1-5). The point: one ought to serve the Lord; the one who takes refuge in him is "blessed" (2:12).

As you walk past Psalms 1 and 2 into the rest of the book, you will frequently encounter the theme of happiness. The word *ashrey* occurs twenty-eight times throughout the Psalter. In every case, it denotes a wellness beyond feelings. To be happy or blessed is a dignified status, a worthy goal. The way it is depicted, one would be out of his mind not to pursue it.

> Blessed [ashrey] are those who dwell in your house;
>   they are ever praising you. (Psalm 84:4)

> Praise the LORD.
> Blessed [*ashrey*] is the man who fears the LORD,
>   who finds great delight in his commands.
> His children will be mighty in the land;
>   the generation of the upright will be blessed.
> Wealth and riches are in his house,
>   and his righteousness endures forever. (Psalm 112:1-3)
> Blessed [*ashrey*] are those who have learned to acclaim you,
>   who walk in the light of your presence, O LORD.
> They rejoice in your name all day long;
>   they exult in your righteousness. (Psalm 89:15-16)

The Source

Now that it's fairly clear that many of the psalms are about happiness, I want to share two observations to deepen our understanding of this important biblical theme. The first observation is that happiness is defined in the context of *relationship*, specifically, one's relationship with God. The psalms are resolute to make this association. Happiness has a source. And for happiness to be, God must be.

> Blessed [*ashrey*] are those you choose
>   and bring near to live in your courts!
> We are filled with the good things of your house,
>   of your holy temple. (Psalm 65:4)

> Blessed [*ashrey*] is he whose help is the God of Jacob,
>   whose hope is in the LORD his God. (Psalm 146:5)

> Blessed [*ashrey*] is the nation whose God is the LORD,
> the people he chose for his inheritance. (Psalm 33:12)

In Psalms, the positional authority of God places him as benefactor. In a short benediction, Psalm 3:8 addresses God, saying, "May your blessing be on your people." Psalm 84 shows him as the "Lord Almighty" ("Lord of Hosts" NASB, KVJ) who blesses the trusting man. Psalm 144 highlights his position as God over people. Those in his favor are blessed.

> O LORD Almighty,
> blessed is the man who trusts in you. (Psalm 84:12)

> Blessed are the people of whom this is true;
> blessed are the people whose God is the LORD. (Psalm 144:15)

Psalm 34:8 further states that God is "good" and that those who take refuge ("trust" KJV) in him are blessed. Thus we are invited to "taste" him and find out for ourselves.

Thus the theology of Psalms constantly points us readers to God (not people, accomplishment, or circumstance) as the ultimate source of blessing. We discover this lasting happiness through a relationship with him.

The Key

The second observation has to do with the *key* to happiness. As we hark back to Psalm 1, we find that the truly happy life comes to the one who delights in "the law of the LORD" and continually "meditates" on it (1:2).

> *Oh, the joys* of those
> who do not follow the advice of the wicked,
> or stand around with sinners,
> or join in with scoffers.
> But they delight in doing everything the LORD wants;
> day and night they think about his law. (Psalm 1:2 NLT)

Torah is the Hebrew word that stands behind "law." It can denote a particular instruction or regulation, or the entirety of God's law.[58] Its more common meaning in wisdom literature is "instruction" or "teaching."[59] Psalm 1 tells us that the person who thinks on God's

Torah is instructed by it. Because God's teaching is his "delight" (the Hebrew noun pertains to "pleasure"), his life is all about doing God's will. An *instructed* life is a happy life.

The linkage between happiness and instruction is echoed elsewhere in the Psalter. You will always find that taking instruction has a positive impact on life.

> Blessed is the man you discipline, O LORD,
>> the man you teach from your law. (Psalm 94:12)

> Praise the LORD.
> Blessed is the man who fears the LORD,
>> who finds great delight in his commands. (Psalm 112:1)

> Blessed are they whose ways are blameless,
>> who walk according to the law of the LORD. (Psalm 119:1)

Not surprisingly, the book of Proverbs, well-known as a life instruction book, shares this conviction. It also associates blessedness (happy living) with wisdom (wise living).

> Blessed [*ashrey*] is the man who finds wisdom,
>> the man who gains understanding. (Proverbs 3:13)

> "Now then, my sons, listen to me;
>> blessed [*ashrey*] are those who keep my ways.
> (Proverbs 8:32)

These verses reiterate a vital truth in wisdom literature: God wants to *teach us how* to live happy lives. Those who heed what he teaches will be blessed. We would do well therefore to pursue God's instruction as the key to blessing.

I close this section with the thought that the psalms speak strongly to us today. In some way, we all desire to be happy. In our search for pleasure and fulfillment, we may hurt ourselves by looking in the wrong places. Many try to find happiness in wealth, power, or relationships. But having all these without a relationship with God is drab and meaningless. Those of us who have sought happiness without him know this. Remove God from the picture and you are left with a fake version.

The psalms point us to the enduring truth that only God can bring true happiness. He offers it to all through relationship—a relationship with him.

Summary Points

- The first word in the Psalter is "blessed," meaning "happy," which gives us the idea that the book is about happiness.

- "Happiness" in Psalms holds a deeper meaning than our everyday use of the word.

- The psalms assert that God is the source of true happiness and that his instructions are the key to finding it.

2. Choices

From how we like our eggs in the morning, to enrolling in a course, to finding a life partner—life is an array of choices. Our lives are shaped by our choices. In the opening of the Psalter, a crucial life choice is addressed.

> For the LORD watches over the way of the righteous,
>> but the way of the wicked will perish. (Psalm 1:6)

> Serve the LORD with fear
>> and rejoice with trembling.
> Kiss the Son, lest he be angry
>> and you be destroyed in your way,
>> for his wrath can flare up in a moment.
> Blessed are all who take refuge in him. (Psalm 2:11-12)

The first and second psalms are partners. Psalm 1 depicts two kinds of people, two ways, two destinies—a very Jewish way of teaching about *choices* in life. Psalm 2 expounds on the better choice: Serve the Lord. Kiss the Son. It is the better choice because those who serve Yahweh and take refuge in him are "blessed" (v 12).

The theme of choices courses through the book of Psalms. Like the so-called wisdom teaching[60] found elsewhere in the Old Testament, many psalms echo Psalms 1 and 2, coaching readers to take godly paths. They place responsibility upon the listeners to be wise with their decisions.

Wise Choices

Wisdom (literally, "skillful living") manifests itself in good choices. Good choices lead to the attainment of a truly happy life, as Psalm 34 teaches:

> Come children! Listen to me!
> I will teach you what it means to fear the LORD.
> Do you want to really live?
> Would you love to live a long, happy life?
> Then make sure you don't speak evil words
>   or use deceptive speech!
> Turn away from evil and do what is right!
> Strive for peace and promote it! (Psalm 34:11-14 NET)

Sounds like a stanza from Proverbs, doesn't it? This is a great example of a wisdom passage tucked in a psalm. The "fear of the Lord" motif appears also in Proverbs 1:7, 9:10 and 15:33. It pertains to reverence or awe of God. Fear of the Lord positively affects practical life. In the above passage, godly fear leads one to avoid evil speech. This is essential for peaceful and happy living.

The psalms advise us to consider *options* when we act and respond. To heed instruction despite opposition is a choice (119:51). To fret or not is a matter of choice (37:1, 7). When angry, you can choose not to sin (4:4). Even influences and associations are clearly matters of decision:

> I do not sit with deceitful men,
>   nor do I consort with hypocrites.
> I abhor the assembly of evildoers
>   and refuse to sit with the wicked.
> (Psalm 26:4-5, cf. Psalm 40:4)

In the same vein, the psalms teach plainly that spirituality does not come naturally. Righteousness does not happen by osmosis; it is deliberated (37:30-31).[61] Pondering on God is a choice (10:4). Confession comes from resolve (38:17-18). Praising the Lord and proclaiming his faithfulness are upshots of personal persuasion (40:6-10).

Similar wisdom pointers are promoted throughout the Psalter. To illustrate, note how Psalms 37 and 84 teach choices by *comparison*.

> Better the little that the righteous have
>> than the wealth of many wicked;
> for the power of the wicked will be broken,
>> but the LORD upholds the righteous. (Psalm 37:16-17)

> Better is one day in your courts
>> than a thousand elsewhere;
> I would rather be a doorkeeper in the house of my God
>> than dwell in the tents of the wicked. (Psalm 84:10-11)

Both passages above start with the word "better" in the English translation. The Hebrew construct uses the common word for "good" (Heb: *tob*) but in a comparative way — there is "more good" in godly choices. This invites the reader to weigh up the contrastive ways of the righteous and the wicked as well as the outcomes of their lives.

What Matters

The psalmists also challenge readers to pursue in life that which is truly valuable and long-lasting. They note, poignantly I might add, that man has the tendency to hang on to what is temporary.

> Do not be overawed when a man grows rich,
>> when the splendor of his house increases (Psalm 49:16)

> Do not trust in extortion or take pride in stolen goods;
>> though your riches increase, do not set your heart on
>> them. (Psalm 62:10)

Such admonitions are always in line with God's virtuous intentions. He wishes nothing but good for his people and he knows what really matters. That's why his counsel is always perfect; those who accept it will be greatly blessed (73:24).

Ultimately, the psalms compel us to give ourselves to God completely. This is a choice we have to make. "Do not be like the horse or mule," counsels Psalm 32:9. These beasts of burden have no understanding. They do not apprehend what their owner has in mind. Unlike them, we should draw near and surrender to God. Elsewhere, we find:

It is better to take refuge in the LORD
    than to trust in man.
It is better to take refuge in the LORD
    than to trust in princes. (Psalm 118:8-9)

I do not trust in my bow,
    my sword does not bring me victory.
but you give us victory over our enemies,
    you put our adversaries to shame. (Psalm 44:6-7)

Free to Choose

God's nature allows us ample freedom to make choices. What determines those choices is crucial, given that our decisions bring real-life results. In liberty there are consequences, and this is where the psalms have a big say. God, in his infinite wisdom, equips us by showing us *what lies ahead*. He does this through the window of the psalms.

We make good choices like the psalmists when we consider the God of the psalmists. Our understanding of God determines our decisions. The Hebrew poets understood the wise life to be a direct outcome of reflecting upon God and his ways.[62]

Yet this is not a dry, mental process. It is not just about logic. God does not want us to behave like robots! Godly choices assume the basic foundation of a *relationship* with God. Knowing God and his ways shapes our choices. The more we think upon God—his perfect character and good intentions for us—the more we are informed for life's decisions.

Summary Points

- The book of Psalms teaches good choices by using comparisons.

- The psalms compel us to go after the things which are truly valuable and long-lasting.

- Our understanding of God equips us to make good life choices.

3. Hope

The psalms speak loftily about hope. Ironically, I type these words in the aftermath of a plane crash. A few hours ago, a small cargo plane suddenly lost control a few moments after take-off. It plunged down and exploded in a village less than a mile from our house! Small houses quickly caught fire. A number of people died or were injured, mostly children. How tragic.

When I mull over what happened, an eerie feeling envelops me. I am reminded that many things are beyond my control. Life is uncertain. And for many people, hope is elusive.

Because imagery is the language of the poet, the psalms offer hope through symbols. Pictures are used to build emotional support for the disheartened. In the Psalter, we are overwhelmed by the wealth of striking images—the mountain, the sun, a shepherd, a shield, sheltering wings—all meant to bring encouragement. They lead us to reflect on hope as a dominant thesis in the Psalter.

The Object

In Psalms, the object of hope is God. Psalm 39:7b puts it in a nutshell: "My hope is in you." God is the source as well as the reason for hope:

> Remember your word to your servant,
> for you have given me hope. (Psalm 119:49)

> For you have been my hope, O Sovereign LORD,
> my confidence since my youth. (Psalm 71:5)

> Guide me in your truth and teach me,
> for you are God my Savior,
> and my hope is in you all day long. (Psalm 25:5)

As a symbol and extension of God, God's word (and synonymously, his law) is also considered a focus of the psalmist's hope.

> I wait for the LORD, my soul waits,
> and in his *word* I put my hope. (Psalm 130:5)

> Do not snatch the *word of truth* from my mouth,
> for I have put my hope in your laws. (Psalm 119:43)

I rise before dawn and cry for help;
I have put my hope in your *word*. (Psalm 119:147)

The Reason

Why hope in God? The psalms testify that hoping in God will not disappoint you. Those who hope and depend on him are "blessed" (146:5). God has proven himself, if you will, in this regard. God is able to deliver (33:18; 130:7). Psalm 33:17, using a military metaphor, insists that "A horse is a vain hope for deliverance; despite all its great strength it cannot save." Physical might is not enough according to the poet. We need to hope in something greater.

Other psalms make the same point by comparing those who trust in God (righteous ones) and those who don't (evil ones). The underlying assumption is, once again, that God has shown himself to be faithful and dependable to his righteous ones. Note the use of the word "but" in the following passages:

No one whose hope is in you
    will ever be put to shame,
but they will be put to shame
    who are treacherous without excuse. (Psalm 25:3)

For evil men will be cut off,
    but those who hope in the LORD will inherit the land.
(Psalm 37:9)

May my accusers perish in shame;
    may those who want to harm me
    be covered with scorn and disgrace.
But as for me, I will always have hope;
    I will praise you more and more. (Psalm 71:13-14)

The Resolve

All things considered, trusting in God is the best choice. The poets remind themselves of this truth. In some psalms, the writer encourages himself (yes, himself!) to be optimistic. Note in Psalms 43 and 62 how the psalmist musters self-resolve to hope in God.

Why are you depressed, O my soul?
Why are you upset?
Wait for God!

For I will again give thanks to my God
for his saving intervention. (Psalm 43:5 NET)
Find rest, O my soul, in God alone;
my hope comes from him. (Psalm 62:5)

But the personal experience of the psalmist leads him to call others to hope in the Lord as well. He wants those around him to gain the same blessing, especially God's chosen people. As David exclaims,

Love the LORD, all his saints!
The LORD preserves the faithful,
but the proud he pays back in full.
Be strong and take heart,
all you who hope in the LORD. (Psalm 31:23-24)

O Israel, put your hope in the LORD
both now and forevermore. (Psalm 131:3)

Hope springs eternal for the psalmists because their hopes are founded on God. In troubled times, they hold to God's promises of protection and deliverance. Even in their darkest laments, they remind us that God will never abandon us.

Have you encountered tough times lately? Do you feel stuck in your circumstances? Are you facing conflict? Take heart in the hope that the psalms offer. Put your hope in the Lord our God who cares for you.

Excursus: The Refuge Metaphor in Psalms

There is one metaphor that particularly emphasizes the hope that the Hebrew poets had: God as refuge. First introduced in Psalm 2, the refuge metaphor underscores God's protective role.

Kiss the Son, lest he be angry
and you be destroyed in your way,
for his wrath can flare up in a moment.
Blessed are all who *take refuge* in him. (Psalm 2:12)

When we submit ourselves to God's authority, he becomes a safe place. The NLT translates the last colon in 2:12, "But what joy for all who find protection in him!" Elsewhere in Psalms, taking refuge in the Lord also results in joy and gladness.

But let all who *take refuge* in you be glad;
    let them ever sing for joy.
Spread your protection over them,
    that those who love your name may rejoice in you.
    (Psalm 5:11)

What is remarkable is how the psalmists take the refuge metaphor in a *personal* way. Yahweh is not just the deity of the nation, but God of the individual. He is a refuge not just for the community, but for each person who entrusts himself. In this regard, there is a vast amount of individual pleas for protection lifted up to God.

Keep me safe, O God,
    for in you I *take refuge*. (Psalm 16:1)

Have mercy on me, O God, have mercy on me,
    for in you my soul *takes refuge*.
I will take refuge in the shadow of your wings
    until the disaster has passed. (Psalm 57:1)

Be my *rock of refuge*,
    to which I can always go;
give the command to save me,
    for you are my rock and my fortress. (Psalm 71:3)

Also, a number of personal affirmations and testimonies come to expression using the refuge metaphor.[63]

But as for me, it is good to be near God.
I have made the Sovereign LORD my *refuge*;
    I will tell of all your deeds. (Psalm 73:28)

I will say of the LORD, "He is my refuge and my fortress,
    my God, in whom I trust." (Psalm 91:2)

I cry to you, O LORD.
I say, "You are my refuge,
    my portion in the land of the living." (Psalm 142:5)

He is my loving God and my fortress,
    my stronghold and my deliverer,

> my shield, in whom I take refuge,
> who subdues peoples under me. (Psalm 144:2)

In addition to taking the refuge metaphor personally, the psalmists expand the metaphor to include a number of other images and titles. At least twenty times, God is referred to as a "rock," i.e., a rock of refuge as in Psalm 71:3. Here are some other terms used:

- "fortress" (19 times, using two distinct Hebrew words[64])
- "shield" (16 times)   • "shelter" (7 times)
- "stronghold" (7 times)   • "dwelling" (3 times)
- "strong tower" (once)

It is easy to see how the motif is amplified in these images.

The pervasiveness of the refuge metaphor is testimony to its centrality in the Psalter. In every use of the literary device, the undergirding conviction is that God brings hope. The poets use words like brushstrokes, painting an overwhelming picture of God telling us to take courage, to hold on. They portray God as a constant encouragement, a helper and savior. Let us praise God, the God of the psalmists, our rock of refuge and our unchanging hope!

Summary Points

- The psalms teach us to hope in God through the use of compelling symbols.
- God is reliable and dependable, so the psalmists testify that we can hope in him.
- The refuge motif runs throughout the psalms and is amplified with several related images.

Questions for Study and Discussion

1. Are people searching for happiness? Explain.

2. In what ways does *biblical* happiness (blessedness) go against the grain of society?

3. How do the psalms help us to make good life choices?

4. Ponder on some difficult moments in your life. How did God bring you hope in the midst of despair?

5. Read Psalm 121, a psalm of pilgrimage. How does this psalm fuse the themes of "hope" and "The Temple?"

Chapter Seven

Jesus in the Psalms

The LORD says to my Lord:
"Sit at my right hand
until I make your enemies
a footstool for your feet."

—Psalm 110:1

MY WIFE AND I have a project, and we're planning way ahead. For our twenty-fifth anniversary, we're collecting pictures to chronicle our married life.

But we're compiling not just the typical photos (like occasions and trips); we're getting *everything*—including moments of giggling, sharing a milkshake, and brushing our teeth.

Although few of you are as eccentric or compulsive as I am, my point is that *pictures speak*. They tell stories. They carry messages. In our marriage, the individual photos serve not just to preserve memories but to convey the big picture, the beauty of our life romance.

The Big Picture

When we read the psalms, the big picture that they speak about is Jesus. He, as the Christ Messiah ("anointed one"), is the greatest theme conveyed by the psalms.

Appreciating the messianic aspect of psalms may be likened to reaching the Psalter's mountain peak. Relishing the breathtaking view from the apex, one concludes, *"Wow. It's all about Jesus!"*

To begin with, consider those who penned the psalms. They are mainly of two kinds: priests and kings. Asaph, Heman, and Korah were from priestly clans. David and Solomon were kings. See the connection? This points to the two offices which are uniquely combined in Jesus, who is both *priest and king* (Hebrews 1:8-9; 5:6).

Previews and Prefigures

Aspects of Christ's person and work are beautifully interwoven into many psalms. In these passages we find advanced glimpses — previews and prefigures of Jesus.

Glimpses of Jesus' Life

Psalm Ref.	Detail of Jesus' Life	N.T. Reference
104:4	Birth: witnessed and worshipped	Hebrews 1:6-7
8:2	Praised by children	Matthew 21:15-16
69:9	Ministry/God's work	John 2:17
41:9	Betrayed by a friend	Luke 22:47
22:1	Forsaken by God	Matthew 27:46
22:7-8	Derided by enemies	Luke 23:35
22:16	Piercing	John 20:27
22:18	Lots cast for clothing	Matthew 27:35-36
34:20	Bones unbroken	John 19:32,33,36
35:11	Accused by false witnesses	Mark 14:57
35:19	Hated without cause	John 15:25
69:21	Given vinegar and gall	Matthew 27:34
109:4	Prays for enemies	Luke 23:34
109:8	His betrayer replaced	Acts 1:20
16:10	Rises from death	Matthew 28:7
68:18	Ascends to heaven	Acts 1:9-11

Like the tiles of a huge mosaic, the psalms contribute to a broad and complete picture of the coming Christ which we come to appreciate when we read the New Testament.

Aspects of Jesus' Nature, Character, and Role

Psalm Ref	Detail of Jesus' Life	N.T. Reference
45:6	Deity and Kingship	Hebrews 1:8
2:7	The Son of God	Matthew 3:17
110:1	Rules over His enemies	Matthew 22:44
40:7-8	Delights in God's will	Hebrews 10:7
8:6	Ruler of all	Hebrews 2:8
69:9	Zealous for God's house	John 2:17
110:4	A priest forever	Hebrews 5:6
118:22	The chief stone of God's building	Matthew 21:42
118:26	Comes in the name of the Lord	Matthew 21:9

Our Lord himself noted the predictive nature of Psalms in his teaching (Matthew 21:42, 22:44; John 13:18), as did the apostles (Acts 2:25ff, Romans 15:9). Luke 24:44 informs us that Jesus spoke to his disciples about how Old Testament passages witness to him.

> He said to them, "This is what I told you while I was still with you: Everything must be fulfilled that is *written about me* in the Law of Moses, the Prophets and *the Psalms*." (Luke 24:44)

The Concept of Messiah

The Hebrew word *mashiach*, from which we derive "messiah," means "anointed one." In the Old Testament, three kinds of leaders — kings, prophets, and priests — were anointed for their special roles. They even used special oil (Exodus 30:22-25). We catch this rare event when Samuel anoints Saul as Israel's new king.

> Then Samuel took a flask of oil and poured it on Saul's head and kissed him, saying, "Has not the LORD anointed you leader over his inheritance?" (1 Samuel 10:1)

In one sense, a very limited one, Israel's kings, prophets, and priests were "messiahs" (lowercase "m"). However, they were restricted in their roles and capacity to fulfill God's expectations. They only serve to point forward in time to something (someone) greater. The Old Testament anticipates one Great Messiah whose coming would initiate a new era. He was to be the instrument through whom Yahweh's kingdom would be established in Israel and ultimately in the world.[65] Under his leadership, things would change permanently.

Like a person sighing in expectation, the Psalter carries profound longing for a hopeful future. When you read the psalms, you get a sense that the poets were always forward-looking. They foresee a time of consummation, when questions get answered, God's rule is unchallenged, and the righteous are vindicated. In bringing their lenses into focus, we find that their aspirations converge on the figure of Christ as forthcoming messiah.

Psalm 118 and Messianic Expectation

Let's further explore this messianic expectation by looking at a passage from Psalm 118, a psalm of thanksgiving.

> The stone the builders rejected
> has become the capstone;
> the LORD has done this,
> and it is marvelous in our eyes.
> This is the day the LORD has made;
> let us rejoice and be glad in it.
>
> O LORD, save us;
> O LORD, grant us success.
> Blessed is *he who comes* in the name of the LORD.
> From the house of the LORD we bless you. (Psalm 118:22-26)

This portion of thanksgiving liturgy talks about the Lord's action to save his people. The "stone the builders rejected" is clearly Jesus Christ. During his lifetime, Jesus applies the designation to *himself* (Matthew 21:42-44; Mark 12:10). The apostles did the same in Acts 4:11. Further, the promotion of the rejected "stone" to "capstone" is an act of Yahweh. "The Lord has acted" (NEB). His deed is "marvelous" and it brings joy. Rejoicing accompanies salvation through Jesus.

The passage also calls a blessing for someone "coming in the name of the Lord." Interestingly, this phrase is used in Mark's gospel at the triumphal entry.[66]

When they brought the colt to Jesus and threw their cloaks over it, he sat on it. Many people spread their cloaks on the road, while others spread branches they had cut in the fields. Those who went ahead and those who followed shouted,

> "Hosanna!"
> "Blessed is he who comes in the name of the Lord!"
> "Blessed is the coming kingdom of our father David!"
> "Hosanna in the highest!" (Mark 11:7-10)

As Jesus entered Jerusalem, the people perceived the fulfillment of Psalm 118. Jesus' coming is about salvation. The ancient call "save us" in Psalm 118 is equivalent to "Hosanna" shouted by the welcoming crowd in Mark 11.

From the triumphal entry we turn to John the Baptist. There is little doubt that The Baptist knew Psalm 118 and had the coming Messiah in mind when he asked about Christ. Matthew records,

> When John heard in prison what Christ was doing, he sent his disciples to ask him, "Are you the *one who was to come*, or should we expect someone else?" (Matthew 11:2-3)

John bespeaks a Jewish hope. It is a historical hope resting on the idea that the God of Scripture (Old Testament) will continue to act on behalf of his people in the future (New Testament). The summit of this rich salvation-story would be the Messiah. "Are you the one to come?" is an all-important question that demands an answer. Jesus responds positively with a messianic passage from Isaiah (Matthew 11:4-6, cf. Luke 7:18-20).

In the same scene, Jesus confirms the importance of his identity as the Coming One when he pronounces a blessing, *ala* Psalm 1. He says, "Blessed is the man who does not fall away on account of me" (Matthew 11:6, also in Luke 7:23). "And blessed is anyone who takes no offense at me" translates the NRSV Bible. Our Lord pronounced a blessing on the person who fully accepts *him* as the fulfillment of the hope and destiny of Israel. Any other attitude would be taking offense at Christ.[67] Later in Luke's gospel, Jesus puts the whole issue to rest by directing the messianic prediction of Psalm 118 to *himself* as he laments the fate of Jerusalem.

"Look, your house is left to you desolate. I tell you, you will not see *me* again until you say, 'Blessed is he who comes in the name of the Lord.' " (Luke 13:35)

A Kingly Messiah

What kind of messiah did the psalmists expect? Psalm Two launches the messianic theme with the notion of *nobility*—Jesus is the Kingly One. The psalmist calls his listeners to "serve the Lord with fear" and "submit to God's royal son" (Psalm 2:11-12 NLT). Here we find the notion of a continuing Davidic dynasty which is reaffirmed elsewhere in the Psalter.

> He gives his *king* great victories;
>   he shows unfailing kindness to his anointed,
>   to *David* and his descendants forever. (Psalm 18:50)

> Your sons will take the place of your fathers;
>   you will make them *princes* throughout the land.
> I will perpetuate your memory through all generations;
>   therefore the nations will praise you for ever and
>   ever. (Psalm 45:16-17)

Psalms 18 and 45, as well as 2 and 110, came to be regarded by most Jews as Messianic.[68] These psalms were composed for the reigning king at the time, but found ultimate fulfilment in Christ.[69]

The kingly stature of Jesus is well-attested in the Gospels. The Magi looked for him as a child, referring to him as "King of the Jews" (Matthew 2). Jesus repeatedly talks about a king who goes on a journey but is sure to return (Luke 19) or a king to surrender to (Luke 14). In his trial before Pilate, he admits he is "king" (Luke 23). More important, the Gospels stress that Jesus is the kingly messiah predicted in the Old Testament.

> "Blessed is the king who comes in the name of the Lord!
> Peace in heaven and glory in the highest!" (Luke 19:38)

> "Hosanna! ...
> "Blessed is the King of Israel!" (John 12:13)

> "Say to the Daughter of Zion,
>   'See, your king comes to you,

gentle and riding on a donkey,
on a colt, the foal of a donkey.' " (Matthew 21:5)

What the people shouted at the entry into Jerusalem says it all. Drawing on words from the psalmists and prophets, they declared that Jesus is the awesome King who is the fulfillment of prophecy.

A Suffering Messiah

But the figure of king is not the only description of the awaited Messiah. Odd as it may seem, *suffering* is another messianic subject in the Psalter. Many psalms depict a righteous person who suffers unjustly. They foretell the passion of Christ, The Suffering One.

As he was dying on the cross, Jesus cried out, "My God, my God, why have you forsaken me?" That's taken directly out of Psalm 22. "Everything from Psalm 22:1 through verse 21," comments E. C. Beisner, "can be understood as revealing [Jesus'] thoughts during his hours of agony."[70] What the psalmist was describing in his own experience centuries before became true of the foretold Messiah. Read slowly Psalm 22 and you will find many parallels with the passion and resurrection of Christ.[71]

Passages such as those in Psalm 22 were used by Jesus on purpose. For the most part, they served to demonstrate that his sufferings were predetermined by God himself. Take for instance the suffering depicted in Psalm 41, where rumors about the psalmist take their toll:

Even my close friend, whom I trusted,
    he who shared my bread,
has lifted up his heel against me. (Psalm 41:9)

Jesus uses this scripture to refer to the one who was going to betray him (John 13:18). Judas was a trusted companion who turned his back in opposition.

Similarly, Psalm 69 bewails unfair treatment. Here, the psalmist bears disgrace and alienation.

For I endure scorn for your sake,
    and shame covers my face.
I am a stranger to my brothers,
    an alien to my own mother's sons;
for zeal for your house consumes me,
    and the insults of those who insult you fall on
    me. (Psalm 69:7-9)

Verse 9 above is quoted in John 2:13-22. As Jesus was clearing the temple, his disciples were struck by his intense passion for God. It was like a consuming fire. Understandably, the disciples remembered Psalm 69 with its tenor of distress and disaffection—Jesus was doing something radical, something that would be seen as unpopular. Psalm 69, like Psalms 22 and 41, point to the life of Christ as one marked by preordained righteous suffering.

The Kingly One and the Suffering One

Jesus as The Kingly One and The Suffering One—doesn't the idea of a king who suffers seem offbeat? Certainly, it is out of the ordinary. But that is exactly what the psalms portray.

To shed light, we could turn to *The Lion, The Witch, and the Wardrobe* from C. S. Lewis' *Chronicles of Narnia*. As the plot thickens, it becomes necessary for the king Aslan (a lion) to suffer for the sake of Edmund, one of the children who enter Narnia. Aslan, fully aware of the rules of Narnia, sacrifices himself in order to save Edmund. This is a powerful rendition of the story of the Cross. In order to bring salvation, no less than The King suffered in our stead.

This is the King I am grateful to have encountered personally. Although I grew up fairly religious, I knew in my heart that I did not have Jesus reigning in my life. I was a church goer, yes, but apart from going to church, I was not living out Christianity or seriously obeying the Bible. Then I met some Christians who introduced me to true discipleship—giving up everything and following Christ out of love and gratitude. I realized the power of the Cross as the main motivating factor for discipleship (2 Corinthians 5:14-15). At my baptism, I surrendered to the King, participating in the sacrifice he offered for my sake.

For Jesus to be our Lord and Savior, he has to be a kingly messiah and a suffering one as well. And that's exactly what he is. He bears a *cross* and *a crown* at the same time.

To sum up, the psalms share the Old Testament's anticipation of the Coming Messiah. Opening up the language of the psalms and exploring their message leads us to a compelling portrait of Jesus Christ, powerful King and suffering Savior, the ultimate hope of the psalmists and us.

Summary Points

• The psalms look forward to the coming of the Messiah who would ultimately fulfill Yahweh's sovereign rule. (If you want to study this out further, I recommend a sequential study of these psalms: 2, 16, 22, 40, 45, 72, 110.)

• Two messianic motifs stand out in the psalms: The Kingly One and The Suffering One.

Questions for Study and Discussion

1. How does it affect you when you realize that the Psalms as a whole point to Jesus Christ?

2. What does Psalm 118 say about the role of Christ?

3. How has Jesus been a king to you?

Part Three

Into Our Lives

Let your religion be less of a theory and more of a love affair.

—G. K. Chesterton

The Bible is God's chart for you to steer by, to keep you from the bottom of the sea, and to show you where the harbour is...

—Henry Ward Beecher

Chapter Eight

Psalms as Life-Tools

I will sing a song that imparts wisdom;
I will make insightful observations about the past.

—Psalm 78:2 NET

WHEN MY DAUGHTER'S BIKE needed repairs, I labored on it with a pair of *pliers*. After half-an-hour of toiling, I took a breather just to scold myself—Why didn't I get that *socket wrench* before when I had the chance?! That would have done the job in a jiffy...I ended up using the wrong tool.

There's nothing like having the right tools to do the things that need to get done. This certainly holds for spiritual things. That's why God gave us psalms as tools. In this chapter we will survey how psalms aid us in some essential spiritual undertakings, ones that have much to do with our lives: expression, meditation, forgiveness, and resilience.

1. Expression

We live in a time of tremendous, rapid change. The frenetic pace of life on earth slows down for no one. As a result, present society is largely *impersonal*. So often people complain of being "lost in the crowd," feeling like a cog in the vast machinery of life. People are depersonalized, disconnected, insecure, and increasingly incapable of expressing themselves.

Psalms are tools for expression, allowing us to break out from society's impersonal milieu.[72] They help us to discover how we feel and to channel those feelings accordingly. They do this mainly by putting into words those emotions we try to grapple with on our own. Then we can talk to God — really talk to God. As one author correctly observes,

> Our habit is to talk about God, not to him. We love discussing God. The Psalms resist these discussions. They are not provided to teach us about God but to train us in responding to him… The Psalms train us in a conversation of language, from talking about God to talking to God.[73]

Roadblocks

What stops us from talking to God? Several factors come to mind. To begin with, we oftentimes are not in touch emotionally. I know this is true for me. Many times I don't know how I actually feel.

How do you express to God your feelings when you can't even put a handle on them? Moods fluctuate. Feelings come and go. They shift shapes and even betray us. But psalms are like high-tech cameras, able to catch anything. Psalms are brilliant in their capture of human experience. And because they run the gamut of human emotion, they are effective for placing our sentiments into *words*. Countless times people have told me about how reading and praying the psalms helped them to realize and verbalize what they actually feel.

Another roadblock to expression stems from our past. Most of us were taught from a very early age to downplay emotion. When we cried, adults told us to stop. When we feared (even of something like monsters under the bed), we were quickly told not to fear. I am not saying that parenting should be permissive. My point is that few of us ever grew up with our feelings being *validated*. Society has a way of stifling feelings.

It's typical to tell others to "get over" painful experiences, sometimes too quickly. We learn to deny feelings. We do things to numb pain. We gloss over issues. All this has repercussions. We can get into an unhealthy mode of pretense. We learn to "act nice" before people, and even before God. Religion becomes a performance. Prayer becomes a show.

What contrast to the vulnerable honesty in the psalms! With gut-wrenching openness the psalmists pen their deepest sentiments.[74] There is no sense of suppression; here there are no holds barred. No emotions are off limits. Even the questionable lines have to be said.

Why, O LORD, do you stand far off?
Why do you hide yourself in times of trouble? (Psalm
10:1)

Strike all my enemies on the jaw;
  break the teeth of the wicked. (Psalm 3:7)

Wake up, my God, and bring justice! (Psalm 7:6b)

Every day I call to you, my God,
  but you do not answer. (Psalm 22:2a NLT)

O LORD, how long will you forget me? Forever?
How long will you look the other way? (Psalm 13:1 NLT)

Say It Like It Is

If anything, the psalms flush away the impression that all prayer must be refined. Many of us have acquired the thinking that prayer should be eloquent, with multi-syllable words. Or, perhaps more common is the perception that you should immediately break out in praise whenever you approach God. That is, you must praise God before you say anything else. This simply is not true. God never tells us to start or end our prayers with praise. Our prayer outlines don't affect God's hearing. And whatever we say, however crude or ugly — God can take it.

Remember that the psalms are prayers from men which were given back to men. As such, they tell us that God expects to hear *everything* from us. God doesn't mind untidy prayers. And don't worry about censorship. The raw edges of life need to be part of our conversations with heaven. God encourages us to interact with him in every kind of situation, good or bad.

The psalms affirm that we are emotional beings; we were made to feel. To be truly human is to be honest with ourselves, with God, and with others about what we feel. At the very least, authentic prayer is cathartic.[75] These prayers move us from being hapless, helpless victims to healing, helping vessels.

Heaven awaits your prayers. Respond to God and express your feelings by praying the psalms. Here are some psalms that can help you on the way.

Psalms to Express Feelings and Needs

When overwhelmed with life's challenges – Psalms 46, 54, 63
When under mental strain or fatigue – Psalms 41, 70
When thinking about the shortness of life – Psalm 90
When seeking brokenness for your sins – Psalms 32, 51
When experiencing affliction or needing comfort – Psalm 22
When needing encouragement – Psalms 27, 31
When disgraced or falsely accused – Psalms 3, 7, 62
When tempted – Psalms 15, 130
When needing confidence – Psalms 61, 91
When feeling envious of the wicked – Psalm 73
When you want to pray for others – Psalm 20
When you just want to draw close to God – Psalm 84
When you want to praise God for his mercies in adverse circumstances
    – Psalms 34, 40
When you acknowledge blessings – Psalms 46, 48, 66, 67
When you want to praise him especially for his grace and mercy
    – Psalms 23, 103, 121, 145, 146

In expressing things to God, there is an added bonus: better relationships with others. Many Christians tell me about this phenomenon.

Somehow, bearing our hearts before God allows us to relate with people in deeper ways. This is not the least because realness and self-awareness are vital for connecting. Thus we have the dual benefit of praying the psalms: it transforms our relationship with God and builds our relationships with people.

Practical Challenges

- As you go through the psalms, try reading them aloud. Verbalization identifies you with the psalmist and helps you to internalize the text.

- When you find a psalm that aligns with what you feel, try reading just a few verses and then "pray" those verses in your own words.

2. Meditation

Meditation is a vital part of the godly life. Warren Wiersbe asserts, "What digestion is to the body, meditation is to the soul."[76] The psalmists knew this well, mentioning the practice in the opening psalm. In contrast to those who adhere to evil ways, the blessed (truly happy) man delights in God's law and uses it for meditation (Psalm 1:2). Further in Psalms it is promoted as a source of pleasure for God and not just the one meditating.

May the words of my mouth and the meditation of my
heart be pleasing in your sight,
O LORD, my Rock and my Redeemer. (Psalm 19:14)

May my meditation be pleasing to him,
as I rejoice in the LORD. (Psalm 104:34)

Parallel thoughts are expressed in Psalm 49:3, where meditation is called "utterance from my heart" (cf. Proverbs 15:28, Isaiah 33:18). These and many other verses all articulate the value of meditation. As a spiritual practice among ancients, it was indispensible.

Old Testament Practice

What is meditation anyway? In modern culture, meditation is characterized by stillness, as if to escape reality or to allow some divine force to enter. But ancient Jews meditated quite differently. The Hebrew word hagah, translated "meditate" in Psalm 1, doesn't mean to sit silent or "empty the mind" as current definitions go. *Hagah* was used for low animal sounds like the cooing of a dove (Isaiah 38:14) or the growl of a lion (Isaiah 31:4).[77] It was also used for human speech, whether articulated (35:28) or not (Isaiah 16:7).[78] The use of *hagah* in Psalms 2:1 ("plot"), 35:28 ("speak"), and 63:6 ("think") indicates thoughtful deliberation. Implied here is the notion of *reflective speaking*. So meditation has to do with purposefully speaking to oneself.

How does one begin to meditate? As a function of the heart, meditation primarily involves focusing on Scripture. This is clear from the basic command in the theme verse of the book of Joshua.

Do not let this Book of the Law depart from your mouth;
meditate [*hagah*] on it day and night, so that you may be
careful to do everything written in it. Then you will be
prosperous and successful. (Joshua 1:8)

Note the phrase "from your mouth," the mouth being associated with meditation. The action implies, in addition to reflecting on Scripture, muttering the words to oneself. As Joshua studied the Book of the Law, he was to repeat them to himself with the end goal being obedience.

Insights from Psalm 77

Psalm 77 provides us with a context for meditation. This psalm by Asaph is an individual lament. It has two basic parts, generally moving from deep anguish (vv 1-9) to hopeful reflection (vv 10-20). The psalmist was distressed, and the latter verses show how he overcame. The change was fueled by meditation (see verbs highlighted below).

> I *thought* about the former days,
> the years of long ago;
> I *remembered* my songs in the night.
> My heart *mused* and my spirit *inquired*. (Psalm 77:5-6)

> I will *meditate* on all your works
> and *consider* all your mighty deeds. (Psalm 77:12)

A devotional reading of Psalm 77 also reveals the important elements of meditation.

1. There is a conscious awareness of God ("I remembered you, O God" v3). The psalmists pondered on the Lord, acknowledging his presence amidst feelings of despair. Attention is drawn to God even through difficulty.

2. Additionally, there is personal introspection. Meditation in the psalms involves thinking deeply about one's own feelings, be it sorrow (42:5), guilt (38:8-9), anger (39:3), affliction (119:78), or surrender (119:48). Sometimes the emotions are pointed, other times the psalmists tend to ramble. This is typical of human expression.

3. Remembrance is another element of meditation. The psalmist recalls happier days in the past or times of deliverance by God (77:5, cf. 42:4). In Psalm 77 the psalmist determines to "remember" God's deeds and miracles (v 11). This of course presupposes an ongoing relationship with God, who has revealed himself to the psalmists in various ways. The psalms assume an *experiential* knowledge of God (119:75-78).

4. Biblical meditation has a "decision element." Meditation brings the psalmist to make a godly decision. At minimum,

it is a change of mindset (77:10-12).[79] Walter Brueggemann calls it "new orientation" in the psalms. The text shows a change of paradigm. And it's not just *within* a psalm that this occurs, but also *across* psalms in series.

These elements point to movement, progress as a result of meditation. As Brueggemann points out about the meditative shift in psalms,

> When the psalm makes its next move, it is a surprising one. Things are different. Something has changed. We cannot ever know whether it has changed circumstance, or changed attitude, or something of both. But the speaker now speaks differently. Now the sense of urgency and desperation is replaced by joy, gratitude, and well-being.[80]

Meditating on the Psalter brings transformation because the psalms commend constant orientation to God's will.[81] When we meditate the psalms, we learn to meditate like the psalmists. As the psalms renew our minds, they re-orient our lives.

Practical Challenges

- Take the *Joshua challenge!* Mutter Scriptures to yourself. Saying Scriptures reflectively not only helps you memorize them; it also allows you to internalize the message (Joshua 1:8).
- Study out wisdom psalms and historical psalms. They enhance meditation. Here are a few suggestions: To ponder on life choices – Psalms 1, 2, 73; to study contrasts between the righteous and the wicked – Psalms 1, 15, 25, 32, 34, 36, 37, 52, 127, 128; to review the history of Israel–Psalms 78, 105, 106.
- Try listening to psalms through an audio Bible. There are several products out there with recording in mp3 or other formats. Listening to the psalms adds another dimension to study and reflection.
- When struggling with sin, recite passages. Remember how Jesus fought off temptation (Matthew 4)? He alluded to the Old Testament, namely from Deuteronomy 6 and 8.
- Recall and jot down what God has done before in your life. Do what the psalmists did by enumerating and writing down past "deeds" and "miracles." Then thank God for whatever you've written down.

3. Forgiveness

The long-standing adage from Alexander Pope goes, "To err is human, to forgive divine." Here the English poet strikes a chord on erring and forgiving. He professes the fallibility of man, but also implies that forgiving another person is one of the most difficult things a person can do. To forgive has to do with something "higher" than humanity. Indeed, there is something divine about forgiveness.

Affliction

Before we speak of forgiveness, we need to speak of affliction. Psalms are fluent in such language. With moving candor they articulate many sorrows, mostly about those inflicted by people. Time and again the psalms speak of wicked men or enemies who "do violence," "trample," or "attack" (17:9, 56:2). Evildoers lie (5:9), bear grudges (55:3) and taunt maliciously (71:11). These adversaries are "vigorous," "mighty," or "deadly" (38:19, 17:9). They may even collaborate against the poet (71:10). In such affliction, the psalmists make no attempt to hide or sugarcoat their pain.

> But I am a worm and not a man,
>> scorned by mankind and despised by the people.
> (Psalm 22:6)

> I am the talk of those who sit in the gate,
>> and the drunkards make songs about me. (Psalm 69:12)

> My eye wastes away because of grief;
>> it grows weak because of all my foes. (Psalm 6:7)

> All the day my enemies taunt me;
>> those who deride me use my name for a curse.
> (Psalm 102:8)

While brooding in their personal hurt, the psalmists wrestle with assorted feelings. They speak of being lonely (25:16) or dreadful (31:11) and having a broken heart (69:20). At times their situations are aggravated by the loss of close friends (41:9; 55:12-14). Just like us, they try to make sense of things, but their emotions weave complexly.

The psalms confess that forgiveness is not easy. What with all this heartache, the most natural response is anger. "I hate them with complete hatred," fumes David, "I count them my enemies" (139:22). Who these enemies are is not as important as the insight into man's reaction to animosity. Hate begets hate. And when hateful feelings overflow, even God becomes the target for blame. Psalm 88:8 captures such a bent: "You have caused my companions to shun me; you have made me a horror to them. I am shut in so that I cannot escape."

Resolution

So what's the difference between the psalms and the usual sad tale? Looking beyond the over-the-top outbursts and poetic exaggerations, what stands out in the psalms is the stubborn resolve to point oneself to God. In due course, all the sorrow and anguish are directed towards heaven. Every pain is "reflected up." At times driven to the point of desperation (3:2; 7:2), the psalmists fight through the fog of pain to keep their view of God, however obscured.

Attend to me, and answer me;
I am restless in my complaint and I moan,
because of the noise of the enemy,
    because of the oppression of the wicked. (Psalm 55:2-3)

I am small and despised, yet I do not forget your precepts.
    (Psalm 119:141)

Turn to me and be gracious to me,
    for I am lonely and afflicted. (Psalm 25:16)

Every day I call upon you, O LORD;
    I spread out my hands to you. (Psalm 88:9b)

As prayers, the psalms are *directed* voices. They speak upwards. With eyes focused on the Sovereign One, they articulate their grievances. For the abandoned, the psalms look to God for the reassurance and belongingness that no human could fully provide. For the victim, the psalms explore the issue of unjust suffering even while insisting that God remains in control during such adversity.[82]

Roadmap

Thus the Psalter is more than a safety valve for pent-up emotions. It is a roadmap to forgiveness. How do the psalms point the way?

First, the psalms meet us at our point of weakness—that place where we are most sure that we have been hurt, that some people have overstepped their boundaries with us. Then, the psalms make us aware of the choices before us, both good and bad. They sensitize us to that moment of teeter-tottering when we actually consider revenge as an option. Almost simulta-neously, they remind us that God is fully aware of man's suffering, yet it is not our role to remedy that suffering.

The psalms jolt us to the reality that righting wrongs is essentially the business of God. In the end, we are brought to a place where we can surrender the most sensitive parts of our soul to his sovereign will. And realizing that we are under God's loving protection and compassion, we can then *do what he does* to offenders: forgive.

Realization

In the psalms, forgiveness is seen as a tangible, realizable state of blessing and favor. God is there at the point when it seems impossible to forgive, and then—if you are willing—he will take you to the point where you can forgive. It may take time to get there, but the psalmists believe, no, they insist that you get there. *They* got there. As they prayed, they were determined that God would bring them there.

As the psalmists sought that place of forgiveness, the prayers they prayed would bring about an inner transformation as only God can bring. Anger and anguish give way to peace and peacemaking. In the psalms, "...torrents of rage have been allowed to flow freely, channelled only by the robust structure of a ritual prayer," writes Miroslav Volf, "Strangely enough, they may point to a way out of slavery to revenge and into the freedom of forgiveness."[83]

By portraying those who find it difficult to forgive, the psalms educate us about forgiveness. To forgive does not mean that what was done to you was acceptable (or that you're "ok" with it). True forgiveness does not condone evil. Neither does it mean you have forgotten the offense, nor that you are moving on easily or that things are "back to normal." Instead, forgiveness is coming to a conviction that you can offer to someone gifts that are undeserved—attention, consideration, mercy.

That only happens when you have surrendered the matter to God. Those who try to see things from God's point of view find it in themselves to forgive, regardless of the gravity of the offense. How this works amazes me. The "divine" perspective truly helps us to make that "divine" choice.

Practical Challenges

- Don't keep grudges. First, tell God how you feel. Tell him truthfully about how you were hurt. Bear your heart. Then, whether or not complete reconciliation is possible, forgive. Remember that forgiveness is primarily between you and God.

- Be a peacemaker. Do you know of some people who are not on good terms? Share what you are learning from the psalms and be a bridge to reconnect people.

Excursus: The Imprecatory (Cursing) Psalms

This brings us to a necessary discussion of imprecations or curses in the psalms. I have already mentioned that based on content, some psalms may be called imprecatory psalms (Latin: *in/im*=toward; *precari*=pray). While most psalms pronounce blessings, these psalms pronounce curses.

Language

Imprecatory passages wish misfortune or call judgment upon enemies and evildoers, often with the use of strong language, as in the following:

> Let death take my enemies by surprise;
>> let them go down alive to the grave… (Psalm 55:15)

> O God, break the teeth in their mouths. (Psalm 58:6)

> May they be blotted out of the book of life and not be listed with the righteous. (Psalm 69:28)

> May his children be fatherless and his wife a widow. (Psalm 109:9)

> How blessed will be the one who seizes your infants and dashes them against the rocks. (Psalm 137:9)

Other vivid examples abound (12:3-4; 35:1-8; 59:10-13; 83:9-17; 140:9-

11). Scholars have identified eighteen psalms that have an element of imprecation—a total of 65 verses.[84] Often unsettling, these passages spawn some theological problems for many Christians.

Observations

Before I give the reasons for biblical imprecations in Psalms, let me first put forward some observations. Foremost, you will notice that beyond expressing personal grievances, the psalmists are preoccupied by a higher concern: They are bothered by evil. "Why do the nations rage and the peoples plot in vain?" asks the psalmist, lamenting that "the kings of the earth set themselves, and the rulers take counsel together, against the LORD and against his Anointed" (2:1-2).

The psalmists are solidly moral people. Never desensitized to sin, they react to spiritual illness in society. And when they do, they think on a different plane. It is not just "about me," but about the damage evil does to the world. So when we interpret their poems, we should see beyond the apparent self-pity or disgust. Imprecations are about moral abhorrence, not personal vengeance.

To *not* be disturbed by wickedness would be abnormal for the psalmist. Evil must be hated, although with a godly indignation. "Indiscriminate hatred is also wrong," Walter Kaiser comments. "The concern," he adds, "must be for God's character and name, not personal vendetta. The hatred, then, is aimed at the evil deeds that are done, not primarily at the persons who do them."[85] The psalms demonstrate to us therefore, what it means to be repulsed by evil.

Second: Curses are prayed to God, not shouted to the enemy. This goes without saying, but it cannot be taken for granted. When the psalms express outrage at the amount of injustice in the world, they grapple with how God would allow such evils to persist. When the psalmists wish pain (Psalm 3) or death (Psalm 55) for their enemies, they leave it up to God to complete the action. The curse is never realized in the act of cursing. In Psalm 137:9 for instance, we find a serious and disturbing prayer. It seeks for the Babylonians to experience destruction *similar* to the one they had inflicted on the Israelites (cf. Isaiah 13:16). The tone is that of revenge. But it is fair to say that the psalmist knew that this would be fulfilled through another agent, not Israel.[86] Thus it is calling upon God to exact judgment in behalf of his people.

In their struggles with suffering, the psalmists strive to go beyond their own little story. They open out. Their concern is wide, wide enough to include God. They recognize that the world is

God's interest. He will right the wrongs; those who withstand him don't stand a chance! "But evil men will die," predicts the poet, "... the LORD's enemies will be incinerated — they will go up in smoke" (37:20 NET). As passionate questions and complaints are hurled to God, there is a sense of surrender — only God can bring about true and meaningful justice.[87] Isn't God able to do what man cannot? So it is best to leave the final resolution to the great Judge (58:11, 75:7).

The third observation follows closely: When the psalms imprecate, they refer to *what God has already done* in the past. Curses are connected to history. In particular, they refer to Israel's salvation story, recorded primarily in the Law or Torah (the five books of Moses). One episode commonly pulled out is the Exodus event, which involved judgment upon Egypt. At least eighteen psalms mention or allude to the Exodus.[88] Consider the following excerpts from Psalm 28:

> Repay them for their deeds
> and for their evil work...
>
> Since they show no regard for the works of the LORD
> and what his hands have done. (Psalm 28:4a, 5a)

The wicked are to be repaid for their deeds. The evil that has been done (v 4) is contrasted to what God has done (v 5). To add, the wicked show no regard for the Lord's workings in the past. They must be torn down. What is the big story here? The closing verses of the psalm reveal it.

> The LORD is the strength of his people,
> a fortress of salvation for his anointed one.
> Save your people and bless your inheritance;
> be their shepherd and carry them forever. (Psalm 28:8-9)

These closing verses call to mind the Exodus event. It was during that time when Israel became God's people (Exodus 19:5-6) and was called God's "inheritance" (Exodus 34:9, Deuteronomy 9:29). The Hebrew word translated "carry" is the same one used in the speeches of Exodus 19 during the covenant at Sinai after leaving Egypt, and as well in Deuteronomy 1 as Israel was about to enter the Promised Land. Thus, as stated earlier, the Psalter presupposes a history; the cursing passages use it as a backdrop. Like lawyers referring to archives to plead their case, the psalmists recall how God has acted in the past to invoke judgments upon enemies.

Lastly, imprecatory passages are aligned with God's character and will. We can count on God in his perfect character to bless the upright and bring down the sinful (as in 54:4-5). This expectation is personalized in Psalm 143:12, which declares,

> And in your steadfast love you will cut off my enemies,
> and you will destroy all the adversaries of my soul,
> for *I am your servant.*

As the psalmist associates himself with those on God's side (God's own people), there is an adjunct expectation that God will convict those on the other side.

The will of God is constant in performing justice. This is why the imprecatory passages only say in prayer what God states elsewhere would be the fate of those who oppose him.[89] For instance, what Psalm 37:2 predicts—that the evil will wither "like the grass"—is found in Isaiah's words to Hezekiah (2 Kings 19:25-26). Similar scriptural parallels (e.g., 69:28) evince the principle that because God's character is unchanging, so is his will. That justice is part of God's character convinces the psalmists to entrust themselves to that will. As Old Testament scholars Hill and Walton remark:

> Psalms as a book confirms that it is legitimate for righteous people to expect God to prosper them for their righteousness and for God to bring the destruction to the wicked. It is never promised, however, that there will be no exceptions to that general rule...Psalms also teaches that trust in the sovereign will of God is proper, whatever one's circumstances.[90]

So the theology of the psalms is based on God's character, which goes hand-in-hand with his sovereign will. The imprecations in the Psalter should then be interpreted as manifestations of that will.

Purposes

Seeing that imprecatory psalms are "not as bad" as they seem, we now turn to the purposes they serve. First, these psalms allow their composers to *express their emotions.* As feelings are put into words, catharsis (cleansing/purification) happens. Hearts are set free. We know this is true from experience. Our prayers today—however raw and reckless—work the same way. God desires and blesses honesty. He allows us to "be angry, but sin not" (Psalm 4:4 RSV). God would rather that we blurt out how we feel than for us to keep things bottled up inside. In the same vein, Apostle Paul stressed truthfulness in the Christian life when he wrote letters to churches (Ephesians 4:25-26; Colossians 3:9; 2 Corinthians 4:2). Honest expression is necessary for emotional and spiritual health.

The second purpose is to identify the petitioner with God. When these psalms wish misfortune on those they consider enemies, they draw a line between the righteous and the wicked, those of God and not. It's like saying, "God, we need to rectify things. These people need to be punished. Here are the reasons and the ways..." There is an attendant tone of self-defense, an implied declaration of innocence. And because the psalmist is "on God's side," the imprecations serve to remind God, as it were, about those on his side. God should defend his own for his own sake. There is a sense that God ought to vindicate himself—meting out justice not only works to preserve his people but his reputation as well.

A final purpose has to do with the *execution* of justice. Imprecations serve to leave retribution to God. In cursing verses, the poets, rather than acting vindictively, ask God to ensure that action is carried out.[91] It is all up to God. Thus instead of vengeance there is surrender, because in expressing anger one gives it up. All the rage and resentment are laid at God's feet.

Interestingly, this is the spirit of imprecatory passages in the New Testament (see Galatians 5:12, 2 Timothy 4:14). Just as the martyrs in heaven cry out for God's vengeance (Revelation 6:10), the psalms cry out for justice. They cry out for "God's action against all the workers of iniquity."[92] This is to be expected by the righteous from a righteous God.

All this should help us understand why imprecatory psalms are included in the Bible. They are acceptable prayers, and God means for them to be included in his Word.[93]

Remember that God is all about relationships. God wants us to talk to him. He wants to hear the voices of our hearts. Sometimes we are angry when we pray. God knows that; he understands that. And he wants us to leave it up to him. When all's been said, the prayer of incense (anger) is incense (aroma) to God. The most important thing for him is that we prayed.

4. Resilience

"Life is hard — and then you die."

I couldn't help but be struck by those words from a bumper sticker. Amused, I saw that the words were true. They resonated. Life *is* hard. We encounter, often with no preparation, struggle after painful struggle. Then we expire. Such is the human experience. Not to be dismal; that's just reality.

The Reality of Pain

In my roughly two decades of work as a minister, I have seen up-close how people go through all kinds of pain. There seems to be no permanent end to suffering, no assurance of eliminating pain. Many times I have stood speechless at the kind of suffering and hardship that people have to go through.

To add, I grew up in third world Asia, by the so-called "Pacific Ring of Fire." That's where you find, not just abject poverty, but earthquake belts and hundreds of volcanoes. I've witnessed the repercussions of numerous disasters, both natural and man-made. But regardless of our line of work or where we were raised, all of us can talk about suffering that we've experienced or seen in others. There is something about pain that makes it universal.

If trouble and discomfort are inherent in the world, it seems they are not inbuilt in our nature. Human nature yearns for ease and regularity. We typically strive for what is comfortable, ordered, and risk-free. How we wish we could control life, keep things on an even keel as far as possible! But life will not yield.

And so we have The Psalms. Instead of giving us what we wish for, God gave us prayers; prayers to pray through the seasons of life, poems to ponder as we navigate the turns. He gave us psalms to build in us resilience — the word refers to "the ability to recover from change, illness, or misfortune." The psalms convince me that God wants people to live, not lives of ease, but lives of resilience.

The Progression in Psalms

I mentioned earlier that The Book of Psalms was purpose-fully arranged. As an anthology, it was organized with underlying assumptions. Much of the first part of the Psalter is composed of laments, thanksgiving psalms occur more frequently later, while praises figure most toward the end. Psalms of elevated praise in series form the conclusion. So lament-thanksgiving-praise is a progression in the book.

Could it be that this sequence of lament-thanksgiving-praise was meant to teach us something about life? Claus Westermann believes so.[94] This Old Testament scholar maintains that the sequence carries theological significance. Lament (petition and complaint) leads to thanksgiving (acknowledgement of answers) that leads to praise (awe and adoration).[95]

The psalms exhibit the flow of the poets' lives, lives which mirror our own. Not all seasons are fun and exhilarating, not all seasons are dark and gloomy. During tough times, we cry out to God. Taking our dilemmas to God, he generously answers. We respond in thanks and praise. Yet it doesn't end there. In the times of praise, when things are good and well, we cannot expect things to remain that way forever. Life is dynamic.

Wherefore psalms orient us with how to deal with life. Although praise is their dominant theme, the psalms leave plenty of room for lament. They accommodate both and in fact instruct readers how to move from plea to praise.[96]

Although the psalms might look like they are in random sequence, they are in fact in *life-application* sequence. Their assorted arrangement tells us that we must go through life's seasons as they come and go. But beyond this, there is a bigger story: those in a relationship with God have movement. They are not wandering aimlessly. There is a goal, a spiritual endpoint in mind. Therefore, we have more muscle to accept life's challenges, more motivation to press forward. God is bringing us somewhere; somewhere better.

Prayer and 'Self-Talk' in Psalms

I want to share another observation: Through their difficulties, the psalmists stay resilient with what we may term "self-talk." While in the throes of pain and even in their most bare ramblings, the psalmists find a way to *lead their own heart* to believe and hold on to faith. It is somewhat like talking to yourself. Observe in Psalm 42 how the psalmist interrupts a litany of woes with a moment of self-examination. All of a sudden, he talks to *his soul!*

> I say to God my Rock,
> "Why have you forgotten me?
> Why must I go about mourning,
> oppressed by the enemy?"
> My bones suffer mortal agony

as my foes taunt me,
saying to me all day long,
"Where is your God?"

Why are you downcast, O my soul?
Why so disturbed within me?
Put your hope in God,
    for I will yet praise him,
        my Savior and my God. (Psalm 42:9-11)

In the midst of the voicing their complaints, the psalmists catch themselves and sort of reconfigure. This is often marked by the word "yet" or "but" (a multi-function Hebrew conjunction). Examples include heavy lament passages such as in Psalm 22. Note the change in tone in verse 3:

My God, my God, why have you forsaken me?
Why are you so far from saving me,
    so far from the words of my groaning?
O my God, I cry out by day, but you do not answer,
    by night, and am not silent.
Yet you are enthroned as the Holy One;
    you are the praise of Israel. (Psalm 22:1-3)

It appears that when the psalmist is able to lay open his heart before God, his faith increases as a function of his *will*. He wills himself to be faithful (self-talk). The process and effect are profound, such that even when God seems far or unmindful, the psalmist is able to hold on to faith.

When my heart was grieved
    and my spirit embittered,
I was senseless and ignorant;
    I was a brute beast before you.
Yet I am always with you;
    you hold me by my right hand. (Psalm 73:21-23)

O LORD, how many are my foes!
How many rise up against me!
Many are saying of me,
"God will not deliver him."

But you are a shield around me, O LORD.
you bestow glory on me and lift up my head.
(Psalm 3:1-3)

Even in passages which articulate suffering, the psalms look to God. This supports the earlier conviction that praise saturates the Psalter. Psalms allow for praise *in the midst of* lament and vice versa. "Pain and praise are simultaneous realities," observes Kevin Vanhoozer. "In other words, the psalmists complain and celebrate at the same time; the theological import is profound."[97] Indeed, the fusion of plea and praise is what resilience is all about.

The God-Perspective

In high school physics, resilience refers to the potential energy of a body after it's deformed. I'm not a physicist, but I can draw some insight from this definition. Some people are able to bounce back, to exhibit energy, after they're "deformed." This was true for the psalmists. Having a relationship with God enabled the psalmists to bounce back from misfortune, to get back up after a fall. Their prayer life, represented by the psalms they prayed, re-energized them.

The psalms train us to grow through trials (not avoid trials). Clearly, God intends trials for positive things. He does not mean to slow us down but to foster spiritual growth (James 1:2-5, 12; Hebrews 12:4-13). If we pray like the psalmists, we can grow like the psalmists. The psalms empower us to do just that.

The key to resilience is prayer. Prayer directs us to the divine perspective in the midst of trials. Psalms (as prayers) afford us a "God's eye view" of what goes on in the world, including our personal travails. When, through the psalms, we get the big picture, we can experience the same effects of prayer that the psalmists did.[98]

In Katherine Paterson's award-winning children's novel (turned movie), *Bridge to Terabithia*, two middle school kids Jess and Leslie create an imaginary kingdom. *Terabithia*, as they call it, is a magical world full of adventures in which the two friends overcome their fears. Because of their exploits in that fantasy world, Jess finds the confidence to help him in real life. That is, the kingdom of *Terabithia* extended to the real world, equipping him to deal with his personal problems. Because of *Terabithia*, Jess could finally face the world.

Isn't that so much like the message of Psalms? The psalms are about the transcendent kingdom of God. Our prayers (*our* psalms), our engagements with the higher world, enable us to live through the hardest ordeals of this world. The reality and power of the higher world stream down to us, empowering us with resilience. Because of God, we are amazingly able to surpass challenge after challenge, far beyond what we thought we could endure.

Practical Challenges

- Read Psalm 42. Study out the role of "self-talk" in this psalm.

- Write down a couple of painful moments in your life. Try to reflect on an aspect of God's character which helped you through those trying times.

- Read through some psalms of David in Book 1 (Psalms 3-41). Take note of passages where you could relate to David's pain. How do you think David overcame his obstacles?

Excursus: When Afflicted by Fellow Believers

"What about pain caused by other believers?"

Whenever I teach on theodicy (God's justice), this is the predictable question from students. An immensely relevant question—some of the most difficult pains to deal with are those brought about by Christian relationships.

When people hurt you, two things are necessary if you want to remain in community: personal restoration and interpersonal connection. Personal restoration has to do with healing your own wounds. Interpersonal connection heals the relationship. The second cannot happen without the first, which is why the psalms instruct us to deal with ourselves first. In fact, personal restoration (Lord, heal me!) escorts interpersonal connection (Lord, heal us!).

Oh, Brother!

When Jesus challenged his disciples to forgive their brother "seventy-seven times" (Luke 17:1-4), their reply was "Increase our faith!" I wonder if I would have responded the same way. We can appreciate how the disciples did not back off from the challenge (to forgive), but they nonetheless captured how tough it would be. When someone keeps offending you, it's incredibly difficult to keep forgiving. How do you keep going when fellow believers hurt you?

How do you build a community in light of the fact that members will hurt each other repeatedly?

In his book *Crucified by Christians,* Gene Edwards explores the agony of being horribly treated by another believer:

> ...being crucified by fellow Christians is one of the deepest pains a child of God can ever know. It can so profoundly affect you that it can mark the end of your life as a practicing Christian. There is no limit to the effect a crucifixion can have on your life.[99]

True words undeniably. Edwards continues with the *potential* effects of mistreatment.

> It could possibly leave you lame for the rest of your life, its destructive power following you throughout your life and on to your grave. On the other hand, it can affect you positively—so positively that when you re-emerge, you are almost a totally different person.[100]

The book goes on to show that in going through such ordeals, healing comes when you *accept* your crucifixion and find the Crucified One. Indeed, going back to Jesus' challenge in Luke 17, the challenge when "your brother sins against you" is not just forgiveness, but healing. Restorative healing is necessary to be God's community of believers. It is not easy, but it is possible.

Enter the Psalms

Four kinds of psalms lend meaning and assurance to our goal of healing. Primarily, the lament psalms interface with our lives as believers, because Christians are not insulated from hurt or pain. Laments remind us that the Bible never promises absolute protection from harm or danger. Neither will there be a clear reason for every discomfort or suffering we go through. We are only assured that God will see us through.

So the laments teach us to accept the pain while hoping in God (42:11), to ask for mercy, and to trust in his presence (41:10-12). We can be glad *even when* there is no resolution yet. That God has seen our affliction is enough. So Psalm 31 prays,

I will be glad and rejoice in your love,
    for *you saw* my affliction
    and knew the anguish of my soul. (Psalm 31:7)

Next, the imprecatory psalms teach us to verbalize our anger to
God, confident that he wants to listen to our unrehearsed, unedited
prayers. These psalms invite us to express our emotions and not stuff
things in. God is ready to hear our sad stories (31:11-13, 35:1-8), so let
it all out. Just make sure you don't leave God out of the picture.

Everyone lies to his neighbor;
    their flattering lips speak with deception.
May *the* LORD cut off all flattering lips
    and every boastful tongue (Psalm 12:2-3)

O my Strength, I watch for you;
    you, O God, are my fortress,
    my loving God.
God will go before me
    and will let me gloat over those who slander me.
    (Psalm 59:9-10)

As we articulate our hurts and pains, the penitence psalms instruct us
to also look into our hearts. It is possible that in the heat of conflict,
we forget that we too have some fault. Here we could ask ourselves,
"What is my responsibility in this?" or "What have I done (or not
done) to aggravate things?" We can learn from the psalmists to be
open to self-examination and correction.

Then I acknowledged my sin to you
    and did not cover up my iniquity.
I said, "I will confess my transgressions to the LORD"
    —and you forgave the guilt of my sin. (Psalm 32:5)

For I know my transgressions,
    and my sin is always before me. (Psalm 51:3)

Teach me to do your will, for you are my God;
    may your good Spirit lead me on level
    ground. (Psalm 143:10)

Finally, the wisdom psalms frame our thinking about morality.
There is free will in God's moral universe. When we get hurt, wisdom
texts prompt us that we can react either in a godly way or an ungodly

way. We have choices; we are never simply "victims." Good choices
pave the way to forgiveness, reconciliation, and healing. These lead to
building community.

> Whoever of you loves life
>   and desires to see many good days,
> keep your tongue from evil
>   and your lips from speaking lies.
> Turn from evil and do good;
>   seek peace and pursue it. (Psalm 34:12-14)

> Be still before the LORD and wait patiently for him;
> do not fret when men succeed in their ways,
>   when they carry out their wicked schemes.
> Refrain from anger and turn from wrath;
>   do not fret—it leads only to evil. (Psalm 37:7-8)

Because life is about relationships, Christianity is lived out in
connection with other people. Biblical principles are never brought
to fruition in a vacuum; God wants us to engage with people. And
because people are fallible, we will hurt one another. We will hurt
others, and others will hurt us. But imagine a congregation praying
the psalms and living the psalms. Mercy reigns and love restores.

The psalms are intimately associated with life, including all its
hurts. As poetry for life application, the psalms feature a profound
sense of direction. The psalms teach us to transpose our anger and
process our pain, such that we are not only reconciled to God but also
to one another. The psalms build community by pointing the way to
healing and connecting.

Questions for Study and Discussion

1. In your own life, what are some obstacles to expressing
    thoughts and emotions?

2. What is the difference between meditative practice in the Old
    Testament and how Eastern or mystery religions do it?

3. Do you find it hard to forgive sometimes? What are the factors
    involved? How do you think the psalms can help you?

4. Read Psalm 73. Observe the impact of the psalmist's visit to the
    Temple. How could this phenomenon be somehow duplicated
    in your own life?

Chapter Nine

A Life of Praise

What will you gain if I die,
if I sink down into the grave?
Can my dust praise you from the grave?
Can it tell the world of your faithfulness?

—Psalm 30:9 NLT

DO YOU REMEMBER THE FEELING of being praised? As with most people, you probably felt significant, appreciated, and valued. Praise builds confidence and buoys esteem. Praise makes you walk taller (and that goes even for short guys like me!).

In this chapter, we will see how the psalms teach us about praise: its essence, its features, and its power.

The Essence of Praise

Our English word "praise" comes from the Latin "pretium," meaning "price" or "value." Originally, the verb meant "to set a great price on."[101] When you receive praise, you are valued. When we praise God, we recognize his value to us; we place great worth on him and his acts. The Hebrew words translated "praise" in the Old Testament carry such a locus of meaning. The verb "halal" for instance means "to acclaim," "to boast of," "to glory in."[102]

Praise is admiration. Praise ascribes glory to an object of praise. Thus when we praise God we give him what is due him. Note that this is different from *thanks*. Thanksgiving is typically a response to what God has *done*, but praise results from knowing who God *is*. It is common for Christians to confuse the two, and to be sure the two ideas overlap. However, they are not one and the same. When you praise God, you speak well of his qualities more than his actions.[103] You can praise God even when he has not done anything yet.

Praising God is giving to God what he deserves. The psalms teach us to do this by explicitly acknowledging God's awesome qualities. For instance, Psalm 48 initiates a call of praise by saying that God is "great." Psalm 71 declares God's praise in recognition of his faithfulness and holiness.

> *Great* is the LORD,
>   and most worthy of praise... (Psalm 48:1)

> I will praise you with the harp
>   for your *faithfulness*, O my God;
> I will sing praise to you with the lyre,
>   O *Holy One* of Israel. (Psalm 71:22)

Thus praise in the psalms is a natural response to God. In praise we salute God and acknowledge his greatness. We praise God because he deserves it.

Praise in Psalms

The psalms are rightfully called "praise-songs" (Heb: *tehillim*).[104] Brimming with adoration, the psalmists saved no ink to give glory to God. Praise in the psalms is liberal and exuberant.

> I will praise you, O LORD, with all my heart;
>   I will tell of all your wonders. (Psalm 9:1-2)

> I will praise the name of God with a song,
>   and will magnify him with thanksgiving.
>   (Psalm 69:30 NRSV)

> Praise the LORD.
> Give thanks to the LORD, for he is good;
>   his love endures forever. (Psalm 106:1)

> Seven times a day I praise you
>   for your righteous laws. (Psalm 119:164)

The Roots of Praise

Praise in Psalms has its roots in relationship. The Mosaic covenant at Mount Sinai (Exodus 19ff) sets the backdrop. There, the Lord forged a solemn agreement with the Israelites.

> You yourselves have seen what I did to Egypt, and how I carried you on eagles' wings and brought you to myself. Now if you obey me fully and keep my covenant, then out of all nations you will be my treasured possession...
> (Exodus 19:4-6)

> All the ways of the LORD are loving and faithful
> for those who keep the demands of his covenant.
> (Psalm 25:10)

The psalms fundamentally anchor on this covenant relationship,[105] one that through the New Covenant (Jeremiah 31:31) extends to us. God sees us as his "treasured possession" (Exodus 19:5, cf. Psalm 135:4). He has "set a price" on us. Conversely, he wants us to treasure him. When we consider him and his ways, we end up in praise.

Creative Praise

Further, the psalms give varied and creative ways to praise God. Aside from the indispensible call to "sing praises" (9:11) and "sing a new song" (149:1), the psalmists also bid people to "shout praises" to God (5:11, 32:11, 35:27, 47:1, 132:9) or to "make a joyful noise" (95:1-2, 100:1). Various psalms reveal a variety of settings, and moods.

- Praise can be individual and intimate, as with someone who gets up in the middle of the night to praise God (119:62) or in community (109:30).
- It can be done lying on your bed at night (149:5) or with dancing before him (149:3).
- Some psalms speak of going to the house of the Lord (134:1) or considering who may enter (15).
- Some speak of bowing (138:2), others kneeling (95:6).
- Psalms 71, 81, 149, and 150 feature the use of instruments to praise God.

Whatever the prescription, praise is based on an appreciation of God and his presence (95:2). God is worthy to be praised.

Constant Praise

The seasoning of praise is never absent in the recipe of the psalmist. Even in psalms that express pain and suffering, there is a place for exulting in God. Take for instance Psalm 22. It begins with a shrill lament, one that Jesus cried out from the cross (Matthew 27:46):

> My God, my God, why have you forsaken me?
> Why are you so far from saving me,
>   so far from the words of my groaning? (Psalm 22:1)

Now compare that beginning cry with these praise passages in the middle and end of the psalm:

> I will declare your name to my brothers;
>   in the congregation I will praise you. (Psalm 22:22)

> I will praise you among all the people;
>   I will fulfill my vows in the presence of those who
>   worship you. (Psalm 22:25 NLT)

> They will proclaim his righteousness
>   to a people yet unborn—
>   for he has done it. (Psalm 22:31)

Remarkably, dire situations do not stop the psalmists from declaring God's praises (see also Psalms 57, 96, 126, and 24). Almost all the laments have some bit of praise in them.

Towards Praise

Moreover, the edited layout of the Book of Psalms reveals praise as an objective. Suggesting a movement from plea to praise, most laments figure in the first books of the Psalter, while praises dominate the end. This arrangement is deliberate.

Like boiling bubbles after a long simmer, the closing series bursts in celebration, such that Psalms concludes on a vigorous high note of praise. "Hallelujah!" (Hebrew for "Praise God!") becomes the jubilant refrain. As Eugene Peterson remarks,

When the time comes to provide a conclusion of the fifth book, the Blessing and the Amen, wonderful and powerful as they are, are dropped in order to bring the Hallelujah front and center as the controlling word. Psalm 150 begins and ends with Hallelujah, but also uses it internally. These hallelujahs are cannonades: thirteen times this strongest of all Hebrew praise words thunders across the earth reverberating the eucharistic end of prayer.[106]

There is an essential message for us here. Just as the various psalms reflect the variable seasons of life, their macro-structure teaches us that we as God's people are progressing. God intends to bring us somewhere better. We too are moving to praise and glory. That is the big picture. The psalms tell us not to get lost in the details. God is bigger than the details. Life in God is better than the details. And so we have motivation to praise God.

The Power of Praise

We moderns might be inclined to look down on praise. Our pragmatic culture can make us results-oriented. If something isn't outright beneficial, why give it time? If something doesn't affect the bottom line, why bother?

Whatever we may think, the psalms assert that praising God is fitting and beneficial. Declares Psalm 92, "It is good to praise the LORD..." Psalm 135:3 concurs, "For the LORD is good; sing praise to his name, for that is pleasant."

See the Potential

What is the practical value of extolling God? The eighth psalm cues us about the potential power in praising God.

O LORD, our Lord,
the majesty of your name fills the earth!
    Your glory is higher than the heavens.

You have taught children and nursing infants
to *give you praise.*
        They silence your enemies
        who were seeking revenge. (Psalm 8:1-2, NLT)

The praise rendered by children is enough to silence those who oppose God.[107] Imagine how the noisy enemies are subdued by the praises lifted from "the mouths of babes and infants" (NRSV). The Lord is majestic and glorious. Regardless of how the wicked assert themselves, they cannot outdo the praiseworthy evidence of God's glory on earth and in heaven.[108]

Power from Closeness

What is it about praise that makes it powerful? Foremost, praise draws us nearer to God. We approach him as we declare his praises. Just as words of admiration bring people closer to each other, praise is one way we move closer to God. I am not saying that God is in need of encouragement; we are simply privileged to be permitted into his majestic presence.

> Worship the LORD with gladness;
>   come before him with joyful songs.
> Know that the LORD is God.
> It is he who made us, and we are his;
>   we are his people, the sheep of his pasture.
> Enter his gates with thanksgiving
>   and his courts with praise;
> give thanks to him and praise his name. (Psalm 100:2-4)

Praise brings us into Yahweh's throne room to fellowship with him. It is not so much about him coming into our presence as it is us going into his. We set our hearts and enter his gates and courts. Do we dare rush into the King's presence? Some preparation is needed if we are to approach the awesome, sovereign Lord of all (see Isaiah 6:1-5). The psalms escort us to meet royalty.

A person who praises God "invites" his presence by preparing a throne for him to be seated on. With God enthroned, the spiritual atmosphere is elevated. The Israelites realized this effect of praise at the dedication of Solomon's Temple. As they lifted praises — even singing lines from Psalms — the Lord showed not only his approval but his divine presence.

> The trumpeters and singers joined in unison, as with one voice, to give praise and thanks to the LORD. Accompanied by trumpets, cymbals and other instruments, they raised their voices in praise to the LORD and sang:
> "He is good;
>   his love endures forever."

Then the temple of the LORD was filled with a cloud,
and the priests could not perform their service because
of the cloud, for the glory of the LORD filled the temple of
God. (2 Chronicles 5:13-14)

Here God's glory manifested in a cloud (cf. Isaiah 6:4, Ezekiel 10:4).
The people saw it and were glad. Israel had so longed for God's
glorious presence and realized it through praise. God the King clearly
made his dwelling among them. What a confidence-booster! Imagine
the elation of the crowds that day.

Overcoming the Enemy

The corollary of drawing near to God is drawing away from the
devil. Think of it like this: God and Satan are standing far apart, both
holding huge magnets. We're in the middle. Depending on our hearts,
we are easier "magnetized" to one side than the other. Praise "orients"
us in a way that we are drawn more to God than the enemy. We can
direct our hearts like the psalmist,

Put your hope in God,
for I will yet praise him,
my Savior and my God. (Psalm 43:5b)

A formidable foe, Satan tempts us, confuses us, and amplifies our
problems. One of his greatest ploys is to prevent us from worshipping
God. Using a wide arsenal, he disturbs and distracts us. He makes us
believe that other, lesser things are more important than praising God.
But the psalmists coach us that only God can satisfy the soul and that
praise is an essential:

Because your love is better than life,
my lips will glorify you.
I will praise you as long as I live,
and in your name I will lift up my hands.
My soul will be satisfied as with the richest of foods;
with singing lips my mouth will praise you. (Psalm 63:3-5)

Praise empowers us to overcome the confusion thrown to us by
Satan. Praise diffuses the mist and reminds us of the value of drawing
near to God and falling on his feet. "Submit yourselves, then, to God,"
James persuades us. "Resist the devil, and he will flee from you. Come
near to God and he will come near to you" (James 4:7-8).

What's Your Focus?

Praise enables us to focus on God. To direct our attention to God is not always easy. Anxieties and apprehensions engulf us. Our sinful natures, indiscriminate thoughts, and the busyness of life all serve to distract us. But praise gives spiritual single-mindedness. It sensitizes us to God's presence, and helps us take our focus off of ourselves and onto him. We then see him for who he really is. So Psalm 22:3, which builds the image of Yahweh "enthroned upon the praises of Israel" (NASB), affirms that God "inhabits" (KJV) the praises of his people.

What a person focuses on mentally and emotionally greatly affects his or her life. We usually gravitate (in practice) towards our most dominant thoughts. Ever been with a group that's there to worship but isn't ready to worship? Praise is the best and quickest way to sanctify the atmosphere. It changes the spiritual climate almost instantly.

What about you? What rules your mind? Are you more focused on God or yourself? Are you preoccupied with God or problems? Consider praise. It works because cognitively, God's attributes are accentuated through praise.

In praise, we call to mind God's proven character; we grasp more of who he is. In praise, we rehearse our knowledge of God, and we come to know him as what we praise him to be.[109] As C.S. Lewis notes well, "Praise is the means by which God reveals Himself to His people." Then we as his people become more faithful and confident. Those who constantly give praise are transformed by it.

God intends for praise to mark and permeate our existence just as it does the psalms. Each one of us is meant to live a life of praise.

Practical Challenges

- When you read a psalm, write down some of the attributes of God that are mentioned. Then take time to praise God for those attributes.

- Make it a goal to find as many qualities of God from the psalms as you can. Write them down. Then consider: Is there an aspect of God's character that I have not praised him for lately?

- Read praise psalms in series (e.g. Psalms 120-134). Note the qualities of God that are emphasized, and then use a concordance to find related Scriptures.

Chapter Ten

How to Study Individual Psalms

Open my eyes, that I may behold
wondrous things out of your law.

—Psalm 119:18 ESV

IT IS TIME NOW to get into the individual psalms. Perhaps by now you can see why I feel studying the psalms is like scaling a mountain. My prayer is that at this point some of you have acquired the personal vision of becoming a "psalm mountaineer."

There are many more forms and rhetorical devices characteristic of Hebrew poetry for Bible students to learn.[110] However, the preceding material should suffice to get into a deeper experience of the psalms.

What follows are steps and guiding questions to assist you as you interpret and live out the psalms. A number of important principles and definitions from previous sections are also restated for your review.

Preparing to Interpret

Bible study is a rendezvous. You are meeting God through God's word, building a relationship with him. It's not just about studying a text; it's about connecting with the Lord.

Each time you open your Bible, you are striving for a spiritual encounter. And this encounter has the potential to transform your life.

As the Holy Writ, the Bible is not meant to be studied only

intellectually, but devotionally. Both head and heart must be involved. Be prayerful in your study. Prayer guides the heart. Prayer makes Bible study a relationship. Remember that exegesis (analysis and interpretation) is not just about aptitude but attitude. Oftentimes the latter is even more important.

God blesses a prayerful attitude when studying his Word. He wants us to depend on him to enlighten our minds and direct our hearts (John 16:13-14). So Psalm 119 implores,

> Praise be to you, O LORD;
> teach me your decrees. (Psalm 119:12)

> Let me understand the teaching of your precepts;
> then I will meditate on your wonders. (Psalm 119:27)

> I am your servant; give me discernment
> that I may understand your statutes. (Psalm 119:125)

One more thing: There is no substitute for reading and re-reading the text.[111] My suggestion is for you to read your "specimen" psalm at least *three* times. The first reading should be done quickly (as you would read it out loud). This gives you a feel of the entire psalm. On the second run go slowly, paying particular attention to parallelism and imagery. Then go for a third reading, this time pausing after each section or stanza, with an eye for how one section leads to the next and how each section contributes to the whole. This exercise of deeply imbibing the text is vital for understanding.

Steps for Exegesis

Appreciating a painting has much in common with appreciating a psalm. We initially look at a painting from afar—an overall look. Then we come closer to examine details, noting aspects about the artist's individual creativity. After this we step back to view the entire painting again. This time we try to take in "the whole message" of the work of art.

In the interpretative process, we come to appreciate a psalm by first getting *oriented*. We begin by asking general questions pertaining to the category, author, liturgical setting and place in history. We then engage the poetry by looking at the creative details as well as unique aspects of the text. Lastly, we "step back" to grasp the *message* of the psalm, contemplating its application in our lives.

Taking cue from our painting analogy, we derive three steps for exegesis of a psalm:

1. Get oriented
2. Get into the poetry
3. Get the message

Step 1: Get oriented

In this step we ask general questions regarding category, data from the heading, and linkage.

Question: What type/category of Psalm is it?

Psalms are of different types. The three major types are praises (or hymns), laments, and thanksgiving psalms. Other categories are festival songs and liturgies, royal psalms, and wisdom psalms. Praises, laments, and royal psalms may be subdivided further. (See discussion in Chapter 4 where I list all 14 different types.)

Notice some psalms are of "mixed types." Examples are Psalm 19 (both a wisdom psalm and a creation hymn) and Psalm 78 (both a salvation hymn and a wisdom psalm). These psalms resist straightforward categorization because they contain elements from various types.

When studying a psalm, ask yourself: *What kind of psalm is this?* This inquiry guides your expectations of the psalm, framing your mind for further analysis. Case in point is Psalm 15. Being quite unlike the adjacent laments, it behooves us to know that this is a *wisdom psalm*. As such, it endorses virtuous character (in this case, pertaining to those allowed access to the divine presence).

Also, knowing the type allows you to compare a psalm with others like it (also in Chapter 4). For example, when interpreting Psalm 111, another wisdom psalm, we can read the subsequent Psalm 112, also a wisdom psalm. Psalm 47 is a salvation hymn; it helps to study this psalm in the context of other salvation hymns. In addition, since it celebrates the kingship of Yahweh, one would do well to read royal psalms with the same emphasis (e.g., Psalms 95-99). You will find that studying psalms of the same category intuitively sets up parameters for interpretation.

Question: If the psalm has a title, what can I learn from it?

Psalm titles or headings provide information such as author, setting, and other directions for liturgy. They serve not only to historicize the psalm (locate it in history), but suggest the way in which such a psalm could be prayed. They could also clarify the theological purpose for which certain psalms were put to use in the community of faith.[112]

Not all psalm titles are generous with data. While some titles are wordy, as with Psalm 60 which has six threads of information, others are only two words long, like in Psalm 25. We saw in Chapter 2 that some good examples for the use of psalm headings are found in the psalms of David. Thirteen psalms (3, 7, 18, 34, 51, 52, 54, 56, 57, 59, 60, 63, and 142) carry information that associates these poems with events in his life. The Appendix has a tabulation of these Davidic psalms.

Keep in mind that the heading is not a primary interpretive tool for psalms. Headings point you in the right direction, but most do not give a clear enough socio-historical setting which is typically the starting point for exegesis. It is the *poetry* of the psalms and the literary conventions they follow (parallelism, imagery, and figurative language) which mainly provide the framework for study.

Question: Does this Psalm have links to the ones before or after it?

Within the Psalter there are smaller, earlier collections of psalms. Close investigation reveals purposeful arrangement. One can find thematic connections among adjacent psalms. For instance, Psalms 3-5 are complaints seeking deliverance; Psalms 39-41 speak of penitence; Psalm 69 and 70 both imprecate; and Psalms 42 and 43 both yearn for God's presence and vindication.[113]

Keep "linkage" in mind as you go through the interpretative process. Many readers look at the psalms solely as stand-alone units. But remember that a psalm may be studied as a separate opus as well as in relation to its group if it has one.

In the Appendix is a list of suggested groupings of the psalms adapted from Fee and Stuart.[114] Other authors come up with their own associations, but I have found theirs to be most simple and practical. I have also added some of my own observations. Note that *not all* the psalms are in a collection. Nevertheless, bear in mind when a psalm is part of a collection, this adds a new level of context.[115]

For the larger groupings found in the Appendix, try to explore the context of a psalm with respect to its *position* in the Psalter. That is, look at how the collection gives meaning to each constituent psalm.

If you are studying, say, Psalm 114, which is part of the Hallel group (Psalms 113-118), read other psalms in that collection to illuminate your understanding of Psalm 114. God's kingship pervades the air in the series Psalms 93-99. Thus, one would do well to interpret a psalm in this series in view of that theme. The same can be said about the psalms in the Songs of Ascent collection (Psalms 120-134).

Step 2: Get into the poetry

Once oriented, you then engage the text by looking at different aspects of poetry.

Question: What are the form and flow of the text?

Paying attention to structure

A psalm is not a mishmash of random lines. Each of these biblical poems was composed with some structure in mind. In Chapter 3 we saw that Hebrew poetry features short sentences called cola, used in parallel (lines) to convey ideas. Related lines of poetry may be grouped together to form strophes. A strophe is in poetry what a paragraph is in prose.[116] Longer or combined strophes are called stanzas. Modern translations commonly indicate the division between strophes and stanzas by placing an extra space between them.

Studying the literary structure of a psalm aids interpretation. As you partition a psalm for closer inspection, the *flow* of the text (in other words, the writer's points) becomes apparent. Strophic outlines can help us to recognize transitions from one point to another. How these points interplay reveals the overall message of the psalm. So in fact, figuring out the divisions in the text goes hand in hand with unravelling its message.[117] By way of example, the structure of Psalm 1 reveals that its message has to do with *contrasting lives:* verses 1-3 pertain to the righteous, verses 4-5 to the wicked, and the teaching is reiterated in verse 6.

Outlining the Text

Coming up with a working outline is crucial. You may ask: Is there a way to ascertain the main divisions of the text? Unfortunately, there is none. Breaking down a psalm into strophes and stanzas is a matter of opinion; commentaries and study Bibles offer different outlines. Most printed Bibles will have some suggestion and these are generally acceptable. Yet there is still much value in puzzling out the text and coming up with your *own* outline.

When outlining, it helps to take note of features common to psalms of the *same type*. As I mentioned in Chapter 4, the major types of psalms tend to share common elements. Pay attention to these elements as they largely determine the psalm's outline.

1. Praise psalms typically have four elements: proclamation, introductory summary, report, and conclusion.

2. Laments typically have six elements: address/invocation, introductory summary, confession, appeal, reasoning, and conclusion.

3. Thanksgiving psalms typically have five elements: introit, call, summary statement, report, and conclusion.

Allow me to give a few pointers when breaking down the text into strophes. Primarily, you want to group together lines with the same theme. That is, lines that have the same sense or contribute to the same thought. With most psalms this is pretty straightforward. For instance, the rough sketch of Psalm 19 has two parts: theme of creation (vv 1-6), and theme of God's law (vv 7-14). A good deal of practice will make you familiar with this step. There are no hard and fast rules.

Note also that unlike Western poetry (such as in standard sonnets), psalm stanzas are not uniform in length. In some cases, the poet does assign the same number of lines per stanza (see 12, 41). Psalm 119, an acrostic psalm, devotes eight lines of text for each letter of the Hebrew alphabet. But this is not standard fare. Some match only the beginning and closing stanzas (as with 33, 86). Most psalms contain stanzas of different lengths.

Finally, you want to be on the lookout for what I call "flags." Flags indicate the start or close of a stanza, marking off a section of text. Psalm 110 is a common example, an introductory phrase, "The Lord." Other psalms employ the repetition of a refrain (see 42:5, 11; 43:5; 57:5, 11). An abrupt change in theme (19:7), including words such "yet" or "but" can also flag a new section, as does a shift in mood (13:3).

Question: What images are used?

Psalms kindle the heart and fire the imagination. They sketch. They illustrate. The message of the poets, it could be said, "is in the pictures." The more visual we become, the better readers we will be of biblical poetry.[118]

When the psalmist claims, for instance, that "The LORD God is a sun and a shield" (84:11a), carefully consider the image. The "sun" conveys light, warmth, and provision for growth among other things; the "shield" primarily represents protection. The next colon (84:11b) expounds the parallelism, so the entire line brings a feeling of security in God's provision and protection.

It is possible for readers to overlook meaningful points if they simply skim through the words without an eye for "picture messages." So pay close attention to the imagery in each psalm, taking note of the parallelisms used.

Digging deeper into picture messages goes a long way, especially when reading about the natural elements and physical features of Israel. Let me explain using the popular ode to unity, Psalm 133. Many Christians read this psalm and fail to appreciate the evocative metaphors.

To describe the beauty and power of unity ("harmony" per NLT), Psalm 133 uses two images: anointing oil (v 2) and dew (v 3). The "oil" in the first image refers to sacred oil used for anointing. It was special not just because of its ingredients (olive oil, myrrh, cinnamon, calamus and cassia according to Exodus 30:22-33), but more so because of its function — the rare and special event of anointing a king, prophet, or priest required extraordinary oil that was specially made.

In the latter image, "dew" symbolizes blessing and abundance in an arid land. The psalmist says it derives from Mt. Hermon and falls on Mt. Zion. A little research reveals that Mt. Hermon is in the north of Israel while Mt. Zion is in the south (Jerusalem and Mt. Zion are used interchangeably). The distance between Hermon and Zion is about a hundred miles, spanning much of the land of Israel! The psalmist declares that the effect of unity goes amazingly from "north to south."

Do you get the picture message of Psalm 133? Unity is rare and exquisite as anointing oil. It is exceedingly precious and its impact is like long-awaited refreshment that reaches far and wide.

Note: At this point of the exegetical process, you might be tempted to immediately consult the "experts." My suggestion is that you go through the 3 steps (including reading various translations), write your own notes as you go, and try to grapple with the text first. Only then should you turn to commentaries and other Bible helps.[119]

Step 3: Get the message

In this final step, you as the reader "step back" to take in the total experience of the psalm and contemplate life application.

Question: What big theme is touched upon in this psalm?

Psalms take up themes. I explained in Part Two how all the psalms point to God. He is the source, inspiration, and communication of the entire Psalter. Also, we saw that individual psalms strum various biblical themes—some nonfigurative topics such as "blessing," "choices," and "hope"; others biblical figures such as The Temple (e.g., 15, 73) and The Messiah (e.g., 2, 110). On a narrower scale, some psalms highlight event-related themes such as the Exodus (e.g., 44, 78, 105-106).

Identifying the main subject/s of a psalm is a vital part of exegesis. An easy way to approach this step is to ask yourself: *What is this psalm about?* That might sound simplistic. However, when we consider that the poets were guided by their faith, convictions, and suppositions as they wrote, this question becomes necessary for interpretation. It is especially important if you want to teach, preach, or in some way convey the message of the psalm to others.

Question: What might be the author's situation and feelings in this psalm?

Psalms sprout from the garden of everyday life. Never floating in a vacuum, they are about real events and real people. Each psalm has a history, a life setting from which it was born. Although in most cases a psalm will not yield the story behind its composition, the fact remains that some situation birthed it. Regarding psalms as prayers, Eugene Peterson asserts,

> All prayer is prayed in a story, by someone who is in the story. There are no storyless prayers...Prayers are prayed by people who live stories. Every life is a story.[120]

To get the message of a psalm, you must try to step into the shoes of the psalmist, to enter his story. Think on *his* story before yours. As you consider his situation and feelings, try to recreate in your mind what was in the poet's mind.[121]

Feelings figure much in this step. Among other things, a psalm is an emotional by-product. Feelings move the poet's pen. Many passages are explicit with feelings. In those which are not, you as interpreter should try to give a *name* to the feeling: Is the psalmist feeling jubilant? Hopeful? Pensive? Depressed? Vengeful?

The identification of feelings bridges the distance of time and culture. Our present situations may not exactly match the psalmists', but we can relate to their feelings. The emotional dimension of the psalms (compared with, say, New Testament letters) is a unique factor which adds greatly to their universal appeal and personal impact.

Question: How would this psalm apply to me?

Proper exegesis steers us into application. The Psalter is not just a book of literature; it is about godly living. We would be remiss to read the psalms and let their impact end with intellectual stimulation or cultural enrichment. Even theological insights, as thrilling as they are, can become stale if they do not produce anything.

Additionally, it has become common for readers to accommodate the Bible to their lives (e.g., using it to "feel better"), rather than align their lives with the Bible. This enfeebles Bible study. The psalms resist such superficiality.

The overall sense of a psalm, understood after engaging the textual details, should lead one to meaningful change. So the conclusion of Bible study should be personal transformation. My own experiences with the psalms have spurred me to change on three levels: my thoughts, my feelings, my actions. This should be made clear in the following exegetical sampling.

Sample Study of Psalm 5

Let's see how the three steps are applied in the following sample exegesis of Psalm 5.

Psalm 5
For the director of music. For flutes. A psalm of David.

[1] Give ear to my words, O LORD,
consider my sighing.
[2] Listen to my cry for help,
my King and my God,
for to you I pray.

³ In the morning, O LORD, you hear my voice;
in the morning I lay my requests before you
and wait in expectation.

⁴ You are not a God who takes pleasure in evil;
with you the wicked cannot dwell.
⁵ The arrogant cannot stand in your presence;
you hate all who do wrong.
⁶ You destroy those who tell lies;
bloodthirsty and deceitful men the LORD abhors.

⁷ But I, by your great mercy, will come into your house;
in reverence will I bow down toward your holy temple.
⁸ Lead me, O LORD, in your righteousness
because of my enemies —
make straight your way before me.

⁹ Not a word from their mouth can be trusted;
their heart is filled with destruction.
Their throat is an open grave;
with their tongue they speak deceit.
¹⁰ Declare them guilty, O God!
Let their intrigues be their downfall.
Banish them for their many sins,
for they have rebelled against you.
¹¹ But let all who take refuge in you be glad;
let them ever sing for joy.
Spread your protection over them,
that those who love your name may rejoice in you.
¹² For surely, O LORD, you bless the righteous;
you surround them with your favor as with a shield.

Step 1 Get oriented

Q. What type/category of psalm is it? This is an individual lament (clear from vv 1-3), meant to call God's attention to the psalmist's suffering. However, it extends itself to include the community (vv 11-12). Several laments carry this feature of looking outward.

Q. If the psalm has a title, what can I learn from it? The title reads, "For the director of music. For flutes. A psalm of David." The psalm was obviously used for liturgy and had singing quality.[122] It was submitted to a *menatseach* (translated "director of music" from the Hebrew), a sort of choir director or music leader. Although we are told that this was David's, we are not able to place it precisely in his life storyline. Any of several episodes in his life could have spawned this composition.

Q. Does this psalm have links to the ones before or after it? The psalm reads like the other laments adjacent to it. You will find parallels in Psalms 3-7. This series pleads for God's justice and deliverance. Psalm 5 is at the "center" of this group and it helps to consider how the whole series might shed light on Psalm 5. Two of the common strands are 1) they all bank on God's commitment to the righteous, and fittingly, 2) they all end on a positive and confident note.

Step 2 Get into the poetry

Q. What are the form and flow of the text? Like most other laments, Psalm 5 begins with an address and plea. David appeals to Yahweh (vv 1, 3) whom he calls "My King" and "My God" (v 2). He continues by describing how he understands God to be: one who is righteous and abhors evil. This section (vv 4-6) is also an affirmation of God's character. It segues into the subsequent prayer of confidence (vv 7-8), which is also a confession of faith—God in his righteousness will deliver the godly. Accordingly, he will also punish the wicked, which is the point of the next stanza (vv 9-10). Note the imprecation in verse 10. Marking the last section is the word "but" (a multi-function Hebrew letter in v 11, also in v 7). The psalm ends with praise in the form of a promise—God's people can count on him for protection and blessing. This sort of conclusion is also typical of laments.

My Working Outline

1. Plea to God (vv 1-3)
2. Perception of God (vv 4-6)
3. Prayer of confidence (vv 7-8)
4. Punishment of evildoers (vv 9-10)
5. Praise to God (vv 11-12)

Q. What images are used? David makes good use of imagery in this psalm, particularly for describing God and contrasting his virtues to the wicked. Yahweh (rendered "my Lord") is first called "My King," a title which invokes images of power, royalty, and majesty. In verse 3, "I lay my requests" pictures a vassal coming into a throne room humbly laying down his plight before a sovereign ruler in whom his fate rests. Other versions translate, "I plead my case to you" (NRSV) and "I will order *my prayer* to You" (NASB).

Aligned to this is the scene of entering the Temple (v 7), which akin to a great palace is seen as God's abode. In verse 5, the power of the throne is underscored by the fact that "the arrogant cannot stand in your presence," implying that they will be prevented or removed. "The boastful shall not stand before Your eyes" (NASB) is the rule.

Further, Yahweh is lauded as a leader and guide (v 8) as well as protector (vv 11-12). He blesses the righteous man and "surrounds" him with favor as with a shield. The word translated "shield" is *tsinnah*, also in Psalm 3:3. It was a large and rectangular one, protecting most of the body.[123] The picture is one of great security in God. Thus the righteous are "glad;" they sing and rejoice (v 11).

In contrast to God who is faithful and righteous, the wicked are depicted as instruments of evil. They live opposed to God. Note the graphic detail: They are far from God's presence and will be eliminated (vv 4-6). The heart of the wicked is full of "destruction."[124] They are deceitful (v 9, "cannot speak one truthful word" NLT). On account of their noxious words, their throat is an "open grave."

Step 3 Get the message

Q. What big theme is touched upon in this psalm? The text reveals an atmosphere of opposition. The psalmist is afflicted. Yet he believes that God will change his situation and ensure justice. So the big theme of the psalm is God's *vindication* of his people.

David's perception of God (vv 4-6) is especially telling. That God is principled and impartial forms the basis of his plea. It is also the anchor for the promise that he holds on to in verse 12. Vindication cuts both ways: Yahweh will deal with both the righteous (among whom David is identified) and the wicked (who are foes to *both* David and God). God's people can thus expect salvation and rejoicing, while enemies will be held accountable, allowed to perish by their own devices. This conviction surfaces many times in the laments of Books 1 and 2 of the Psalter.

Q. What might be the author's situation and feelings in this psalm?
It is impossible to determine the original context of the psalm. As
mentioned, a number of episodes in David's life could have birthed
Psalm 5.

At any rate, the psalm arose out of opposition by enemies (cf.
Psalms 3, 4). There is an air of discouragement and despair. Reflecting
on his misfortune, the poet is in "meditation" (KJV). The word in verse
1 refers to inner thoughts, hence "sighing" in the NIV ("groaning"
NASB, ESV; "inmost thoughts" NEB). It seems the psalmist has been
falsely accused (vv 6, 9) or disgraced (vv 4, 10), and he is deeply
affected. The situation has apparently dragged on. Understandably,
he is wrestling with feelings of despondency, hatred, and vengeance.

Q. How would this psalm apply to me? Psalm 5 harps on the tough
times in life—fierce opposition, debilitating affliction, grinding
discouragement... We all experience these; we can relate to the
psalmist's poignant cry for help. And we can also learn from his
relationship with God.

As a victim of injustice, David seeks an audience with the King.
His dialogue with heaven changes him. Like so many laments, there
is movement from plea (vv 1-3) to praise (vv 11-12). The change we
see is dramatic and inspiring, a transformation made possible by a
firm understanding of God. This leads us to consider *three points of life
application.*

1. We can pray honestly and humbly.

David was determined to bring his case to Yahweh. Not minding
repeating himself (vv 1-2), he implores the Lord in plain but persuasive
terms. We would do well to pray like David. God wants us to bare
our hearts before him, to spell out our feelings and not hold back.
And God doesn't mind if we replay some of our prayers. It shows
humility and faith. Didn't our Lord make this point in the Parable of
the Persistent Widow? Luke tells us that Jesus spoke that parable "to
the effect that they *ought always to pray* and not lose heart" (Luke 18:1
ESV).

2. We can pray with pointed expectation.

David expresses hope in the midst of despair. His against-all-
odds-expectant attitude is worth emulating. Just like David, we can
eagerly approach Yahweh's throne and before him "lay our requests"

(v 3, literally, "make an order"). "I will order *my prayer* to You," translates the NASB. To the poet, prayer is like "making an order." This denotes being unambiguous in prayer and being clear in your mind that God will answer.

Note also how David prayed in the *morning* (v 3) and would eagerly watch (literally, "look forward") to see God's answer as he went through his day. "Morning" in this psalm represents renewal and a fresh faith. Lamentations 3:22-24 conveys the same thought. It's a good thing to start your day by bringing your specific concerns to God and anticipate his response. The model of praying early and waiting on God through the day makes for a healthy spiritual pattern. Jesus did the same (Mark 1:35-39).

3. We can remain righteous in affliction.

How do we react in affliction? Are we quick to retaliate? David reminded himself of God's character while he prayed (vv 4-6). This is a crucial point for righteousness. As we remind ourselves of God's perfection, especially his perfect justice, we are led to seek him for vindication. We are not to exact revenge for ourselves (Romans 12:17-19). Instead, we can be self-controlled and forbearing as we take hold of the promises of God (v 12).

Like other psalms which also rehearse God's awesome qualities, Psalm 5 prompts us that those who love the Lord's "name" will rejoice in it — the terms "name" and "your name" are found over 100 times in the Psalter and refer to the totality of God's attributes. We can *pray* Psalm 5 in a personal way by recounting God's works and who he is to us. Keeping who God is before us gives a higher perspective in life, affording a spiritual dimension that is necessary to stay righteous in troubled times.

Questions for Study and Discussion

* How do the psalms develop our concept of God?
* How do the psalms change the way we think?
* How might the psalms help us grow in our relationships?
* What are some ways that Psalms can make a practical difference in your life?

Summary Points

- The three steps and guide questions for working through the text are:

Step 1 Get oriented
Q. What type/category of psalm is it?
Q. If the psalm has a title, what can I learn from it?
Q. Does this psalm have links to the ones before or after it?

Step 2 Get into the poetry
Q. What are the form and flow of the text?
Q. What images are used?

Step 3 Get the message
Q. What big theme is touched upon in this psalm?
Q. What might be the author's situation and feelings in this psalm?
Q. How would this psalm apply to me?

- The psalms cannot be divorced from making a difference in our thinking, feelings, and actions. They were meant to powerfully change our lives.

Conclusion

Psalms and Life-Change

PSALMS ARE TRUE TO LIFE. We know this because through the ages, music and poetry were vital channels by which people expressed themselves. It is through song and verse that people contemplated, conversed and connected. Through lyrics, some of man's most acute emotions and deepest insights found expression.

For Life

The psalms truly reflect life. They comprise a mixed compendium. They are not formulaic in their ordering. Their subjects and tones vary to great extents. They surprise you. Sometimes the poets prognosticate, sometimes they vacillate. And the layers and textures of their writings reflect the many complexities of our own existence.

But the message of the psalms goes much further than relating to human behavior or experience. God has bequeathed the Psalter to make a difference in our lives. No, not just to "feel good" when we're down. Not just to find some shallow assurance that things will "get better." The psalms point us to a God who is concerned about how we live.

As with the whole of Scripture, God intends for the psalms to profoundly influence us and shape the way we live. The psalms challenge us to change. They resist dull comfort. They break clichés. They compel us to strive for newness.

Life-Change

To appropriate the psalms into our lives would mean some of the following:

1. Change in the way we view God, especially growing in appreciation of his divine attributes made known in the psalms.

2. Change in the way we see Jesus, especially noting that he is the foretold Messiah, the anticipated deliverer and instrument of God's reign.

3. Change in the way we pray, especially after observing how the psalmists prayed with passion and vulnerability.

4. Change in our priorities, including how we use our time and finances, especially upon seeing how the Psalter treats the fleeting nature of life.

5. Change in our patterns of obedience, especially in light of the psalms' insistence that following godly principles are for our best interests.

6. Change in how we forgive others, especially when we have already "prayed up" our anger, and when the psalms create a group culture where we surrender and submit all our feelings to God.

7. Change in our outlook towards suffering, especially from the transcendence taught and demonstrated by the psalmists through their afflictions.

8. Change in our attitude regarding sin, particularly to shun it, especially as we imitate the psalmists' tenacity to adhere to righteousness.

9. Change in our devotion to God's people, especially after seeing how God desires to fellowship with people and build a worshipful community.

10. Change in our appreciation of God's word, especially capturing the way the psalmists revered and studied it, inspiring us to stand in awe before the Author.

As you consistently read and apply the psalms, I am confident that you will see these changes. Change is powerful and change brings glory to God.

As you so pray and desire, the Lord of the psalmists will open up his inexhaustible well of scriptural understanding that leads to growth and blessing.

My prayer is that as you get into the psalms, they will move you, humble you, captivate you, and change you, to draw near and become more like the Christ Messiah of whom they speak.

May the message of the psalms inspire us.

May their story invade us.

May their power be among us.

Glossary

acknowledgement psalms. See thanksgiving psalms.

anthropomorphic. A literary device that uses anthropomorphism, meaning, portraying something as a person. In the psalms, God is described as if he were a person.

benediction. A prayer for or declaration of blessing.

colon. In Hebrew poetry, a phrase or short sentence (usually paired with another).

communal/national praise psalm. A psalm reporting that God has acted on behalf of the community. It is usually in response to a specific event that has just occurred.

complaint psalm. Another name for lament psalm. This type of psalm expresses sorrow and pleads for divine intervention.

creation hymn. A praise psalm that marvels at God's creative power or sovereignty over creation. It may invoke some reflection on creation.

cursing psalms. See imprecatory psalms.

didactic psalms (wisdom psalms/ songs). Psalms designed to impart teaching (didactic=meant for instruction). They typically contain instruction for or abstractions about life.

doxology. From the Greek, doxa=praise, logos=word/matter, a passage or insert which praises God.

emblematic parallelism. A variation of synthetic parallelism where one line explains the emblem in another.

enthronement psalms. Poems that visualize the kingship of the Lord and were probably part of an actual festival of enthronement.

exegesis. A process of examination by which one comes to understand a particular passage of Scripture. Simply put, analysis and interpretation.

figures of speech. Occurs when a word or phrase is used in a sense other than the usual or literal sense.

general hymns. A song of praise. Hymns extol God for a great variety of reasons, chiefly his majesty and perfect character.

genre. A kind or type, used in the literary and musical arts.

individual praise psalm. A psalm offered by an individual worshipper rather than a group.

imprecations. From the Latin, im=against and precari=pray, passages which call misfortune or harm upon others (see imprecatory psalms).

imprecatory psalms. A type of psalm which calls curses or wishes misfortune upon enemies.

hymn. Another term for psalm of praise.

lament psalms. A psalm which primarily expresses of sorrow or loss.

line. In Hebrew poetry, a combination of two or more cola.

liturgical psalm. A psalm used in public ceremony or services of worship.

messianic psalm. A psalm which predicts or depicts the coming of the messiah in the person of Jesus Christ.

parallelism. A distinctive of Hebrew poetry, where cola (short sentences) are combined in parallel to make a point or deliver an idea.

petition psalms. Psalms which convey requests for deliverance or strength.

pilgrimage psalms (Songs of Ascent or Songs of Degrees). Refers to Psalms 120-134; psalms associated with Israel's pilgrimage from Exodus to Canaan or with the annual pilgrimage to the Temple.

psalms of penitence (or prayer songs of the sinner). Psalms which reflect the sinfulness of man, typically articulating guilt and remorse.

prayers for deliverance. Lament psalms which elaborate on a grave situation (more details given compared to general complaints).

prosody. Refers to poetic structure and composition.

salvation hymns. Psalms which praise God as Lord of History, recounting his salvific acts.

songs of ascent. See pilgrimage psalms.

songs of confidence. Psalms that emphasize assurance and trust in God, as well as affirm God's faithfulness (also called songs of trust).

songs of Zion. Psalms that eulogize God's presence in the royal city, Jerusalem (Zion is a hill in that city), and give praise to the city itself.

stanzas. Longer or combined strophes.

strophe. A series of related lines of poetry. A strophe is in poetry what a paragraph is in prose.

superscription. The heading or title of a psalm, usually printed just above the first verse.

thanksgiving psalms (or acknow-ledgement psalms). Psalms that express thanks to God in response to some positive action or circumstance.

wisdom psalm. See didactic psalm.

Note: This glossary does not include all technical literary terms, since most are defined in context and are not used elsewhere.

APPENDIX A
Psalm Linkages and Smaller Collections*

Collection	Description
Psalms 1-2	Introduction to the entire Psalter. Psalm 1 serves as a preface while Psalm 2 announces its messianic theme. The word "blessed" frames the two psalms (1:1; 2:12).
Psalms 3-7	Five pleas for help. Psalms 3, 5, and 7 plead for deliverance from foes, while 4 pleads for relief in time of drought and 6 for healing. Note the internal links (e.g., compare 3:5 with 4:8 and 3:7 with 6:4, 7:1).
Psalms 9-13	Laments for deliverance of the righteous poor; the helpless person is a victim of social injustice. Psalms 9 and 10 form an acrostic: successive lines beginning with the letters of the Hebrew alphabet in sequence.
Psalms 15-24	On access to the Temple. The outer frame (15 and 24) has the same basic question: Who has access to Yahweh's Temple (15:1; 24:3)? 16 and 23 express trust in Yahweh; 17 and 22 plead for deliverance.
Psalms 34-37	Instruction in godly wisdom. Note the warnings to remain righteous even in trouble and affliction. 34 and 37 are alphabetic acrostics.
Psalms 38-41	Confession songs. The trouble (illness in 3 cases) is due to sin. The psalmist seeks brokenness and appeals for mercy. See also Psalm 51.
Psalms 46-48	On the celebration of Zion (Jerusalem). 46 and 48 converse on security in Zion, 47 on Yahweh's kingship over all the earth.
Psalms 60-64	Five prayers with common themes, enclosed by a community lament (60) and an individual lament (64). They are spoken by/of the king, on the importance of Yahweh's presence and protection.
Psalms 73-78	Rejection and Hope for Zion. As with Book 1, a wisdom psalm opens Book 3. Psalm 78, which closes the series, is also a wisdom psalm. Question is tackled: Will the Lord reject us? What are his plans for us?

Psalms 79-83   How long? is a question that lingers in these psalms (79:5; 80:4). God's faithfulness is "put to the test." God seems distant and uninvolved. The psalmists call: Rise up, do not be silent (82:8; 83:1).

Psalms 90-92   Yahweh is our dwelling place. Psalms 73 and 90 are like "two poles" on which the theology of the psalms is anchored (Terrien). Security and faith in God are highlighted.

Psalms 93-99   A series of praise psalms. The apparent exception (94) nonetheless assumes Yahweh's reign as it calls for justice on those who reject Yahweh's law.

Psalms 100-106   Praise of Yahweh is continued. Some of the most profound expressions of praise are lifted up here.

Psalms 110-118   The coming King is put forward in 110. The series is framed by two royal psalms 110 and 118. Some consider 113-118 as a separate collection of Hallel (praise psalms).

Psalms 120-134   God is over history. Excerpts of the story of Israel are found here. Many of these Psalms of Ascent (Songs of Degrees) would have been sung during ceremonial processions to the Temple.

Psalms 135-137   Response to the Ascents. Note the crescendo of praise that is building up. These were associated with David and Levitical singing.

Psalms 138-145   The Final Davidic Collection. Some consider this series as a fruit of David's gratitude and sense of purpose as he takes the throne (138:8). It also recounts some of the troubles he went through before his reign.

Psalms 146-150   A Fivefold Hallelujah which serves as the final benediction. A fitting conclusion not just to the fifth book but to the entire Psalter.

*Adapted from *How to Read the Bible Book by Book* (see endnote). Note: not all of the 150 psalms belong to a group or have clear linkage to adjacent psalms.

APPENDIX B
Books for Further Reading

On Hebrew Poetry and Wisdom Literature

Alter, R. *The Art of Biblical Poetry.* New York: Basic Books, 1985.

Murphy, Roland E. *The Tree of Life: An Exploration of Biblical Wisdom Literature.* Grand Rapids, MI: Eerdmans, 1997; New York: Doubleday, 1990.

Petersen, David L. and Kent Harold Richards, *Interpreting Hebrew Poetry.* Minneapolis: Fortress, 1992.

Von Rad, Gerhard. *Wisdom in Israel.* London: SCM, 1970.

On the Psalms

Allen, Leslie C. *Psalms 101-150.* Word Biblical Commentary. Dallas, TX: Word, 2002.

Broyles, Craig C. *Psalms.* New International Biblical Commentary. Peabody, MA: Hendrickson, 1999.

Brueggemann, Walter. *The Spirituality of the Psalms.* Minneapolis, MN: Augsburg Fortress, 2001.

Craigie, Peter C. *Psalms 1-50.* Word Biblical Commentary. Dallas, TX: Word, 1983.

Lewis, C.S. *Reflections on the Psalms.* New York: Harcourt Brace & Co., 1958.

McCann, J. Clinton. *A Theological Introduction to the Book of Psalms.* Nashville, TN: Abingdon, 1993.

APPENDIX C

Psalms of David and Connected Narratives

Chapter in the Psalms	Narrative in David's Life	Description
(Psalm) 59	1 Samuel 19:8-18	Saul, in a fit of jealousy, tries to kill David. By a thread he escapes, through no less than Saul's daughter Michal.
56, 34	1 Samuel 21:10-15	David, fearing for his life, pretends to be a madman. The acting job seems to have worked, since Achish was convinced. David is spared and he praises God for it.
142	1 Samuel 22:1-3	After being cast out by Achish, David flees to Adullam. Hiding in a cave, he is downcast and overwhelmed.
52	1 Samuel 22:9-23	At Saul's command, Doeg the Edomite commits mass murder. David is saddened over such wickedness.
63	1 Samuel 23:14	In 1 Samuel 23 and 24, David continues to flee from Saul. He hides in various "strongholds" in the desert. In 2 Samuel 15, Absalom's following has grown, causing David to flee. The people of the countryside weep seeing their deposed king.
54	1 Samuel 23:19-29	The Ziphites went to Saul and told him that David was hiding amongst them. They told him exactly where they could locate David, but God delivered him out of the king's hands.
57	1 Samuel 24:1-22	In En Gedi, Saul was in hot pursuit of David. When Saul was caught in a compromised position, David could have killed him, but did not, proving that he was more merciful that Saul. (It is possible that Psalms 52 and 57 refer to the same event.)
7	1 Samuel 24:9-12	It was possibly Cush the Benjamite who had been feeding Saul with lies about David. He told Saul that David had been seeking to kill him all along.
60	2 Samuel 8:13	David lifts up God for granting a massive victory over the Edomites.
51	2 Samuel 11-12	Along with David's sin of adultery with Bathseba, he committed abuse of authority and murder. David repents after a rebuke from Nathan.
3	2 Samuel 15	Absalom rebels against his father David. This, among many family troubles, resulted from his sin with Bathsheba. David flees Jerusalem.
18	1 Samuel 24 and 26	David is delivered from Saul. Psalm 18 seems to be a composition regarding all of God's acts of deliverance. See also 2 Samuel 22.

End Notes

CHAPTER 1: SONGS OF GREAT WORTH

1. The Hebrew verb *zamar* means "to sing or make music" or "to play on strings." The related noun *mizmor*, meaning "song," is found in the heading of 57 psalms. This designation is apparently taken as characteristic of the majority of the collection.

2. The hymn was sung antiphonally: Jesus as the leader would sing the lines, and his followers would respond with "Hallelujah!" Parts of it must have been deeply moving to the disciples when after the Resurrection they remembered that Jesus sang words pledging that he would keep his vows (116:12-13), ultimately triumph despite rejection (118), and call all nations to praise the Lord and his covenant love (117). Donald A. Carson, "Matthew," *Zondervan NIV Bible Commentary*, Kenneth Barker and John Kohlenberger III, eds. (Grand Rapids: Zondervan, 1994; Pradis Electronic Version produced by Zondervan Interactive, 2002). Hereafter, *Zondervan NIV Bible Commentary* shall be referred to as *ZNBC*.

3. W. L. Holladay, *The Psalms Through Three Thousand Years: Prayer Book of a Cloud of Witnesses* (Minneapolis: Fortress, 1993), 161-190, cited in Samuel L. Terrien, *The Psalms: Strophic Structure and Theological Commentary*, (Grand Rapids: Eerdmans, 2003), 1-2.

4. *New International Bible Dictionary*, J. D. Douglas, rev. ed. (Grand Rapids: Zondervan, 1997; Pradis Electronic Version produced by Zondervan Interactive, 2002), s.v. "Book of Psalms." Hereafter, *New International Bible Dictionary* shall be referred to as *NIBD*.

5. The plural *psalmoi* meant "twangings [of harp strings]" and so songs sung to harp accompaniment. Ibid. Another tradition also shows the title *psalterion*, "a stringed instrument," possibly a harp. Terrien, 10, 29.

6. S.R. Driver, *An Introduction to the Literature of the Old Testament* (N.Y.: Meridian books, 1956), 367. See also John Eaton, *The Psalms: A Historical and Spiritual Commentary* (N.Y.: Continuum International, 2005), 10.

CHAPTER 2: BACKGROUND OF PSALMS

7. This was foreseen in Deuteronomy 12:5-7. Albert C. Knudson, *The Religious Teaching of the Old Testament* (N.Y.: Abingdon Press, 1918), 34. The regular pilgrimage to Jerusalem (Deuteronomy 16:16;

31:11) also meant regular visits to the Temple.

8. Scholars tell us that close investigation has proved that in all religions, Christianity included, religious poetry has originated in connection with congregational worship, and has been subordinated to it. What is unique about the Psalms is how these reflect the national character and religion of Israel. Driver, 361. Driver established early on that many of the psalms in the Psalter have been used in the cult of the Second Temple. S. Mowinckel, *The Psalms in Israel's Worship* (Oxford: Blackwell, 1962 reprinted Grand Rapids, MI: Eerdmans, 2004), 2-11.

9. I do not want to lightly dismiss the centuries of debate regarding authorship of the psalms. The issues are inexorably connected to how psalm titles are to be interpreted. See *NIBD*, s.v. "Book of Psalms."

10. Based on headings alone. Note that Psalm 88 has "shared" authorship (Heman and Korahites).

11. The Jewish Talmud attributes all the psalms to David. C. Hassell Bullock, *Encountering the Book of Psalms* (Grand Rapids: Baker, 2001), 23.

12. These are Psalms 2, 16, 32, 69, 95, and 110 (see Acts 4:25, Acts 2:31, Romans 4:6, Romans 11:9, Hebrews 4:7, and Matthew 22:43). Elsewhere, Jewish writings have no consensus on Davidic authorship. *Baba Bathra* mentions ten while *Pesachim* attributes all the Psalms to David.

13. It is inconclusive whether each psalm of this group was *jointly* composed by all the sons of Korah — better to surmise that some clan members had compositions and others compiled them.

14. Numbering also varies in the Greek and Hebrew versions. E.g., Psalms 9 and 10 in the Hebrew are fused to make Psalm 9 in the Greek Bibles, Psalms 114 and 115 in the Hebrew are fused to make Psalm 113. Protestant Bibles tend to follow the Hebrew version, Catholic Bibles the Greek version. Gordon D. Fee and Douglas Stuart, *How to Read the Bible Book by Book* (Grand Rapids: Zondervan, 2002), 130.

15. Before it was translated into Greek (at least two hundred years before Christ), The Psalms had already been edited and arranged. Luke shows awareness of their numbering in the expression "the second psalm" (Acts 13:33).

16. Thematic parallels with the Pentateuch are striking and make for good Bible study: Book 1 and Genesis — God's blessing, creation, rebellion, redemption. Book 2 and Exodus--hardship, deliverance, backsliding. Book 3 and Leviticus--holiness and God's Sanctuary. Book 4 and Numbers--pilgrimage and anticipated rest. Book 5 and

Deuteronomy--instruction, obedience, and blessing. Not surprisingly, the Jewish interpreter Saadia Gaon (c. 882-942) viewed the Psalter as a second Pentateuch. Mowinckel, xxi.

17. Only thirty-four psalms are untitled: Psalms 1, 2, 10, 33, 43, 71, 91, 93, 94, 95, 96, 97, 99, 104, 105, 106, 107, 111, 112, 113, 114, 115, 116, 117, 118, 119, 135, 136, 137, 146, 147, 148, 149, 150.

18. This assertion deserves a whole chapter, but one could start by considering the hymn (psalm) in Habakkuk 3, where the title is considered part of the canonical text.

19. The titles are counted in the versification of the Hebrew text but not in the English translation. Thus the numbers in Hebrew lag by a verse (or two). For example, Psalm 46:1 in traditional English texts is Psalm 46:2 in Hebrew. See Gleason L. Archer, Jr., *A Survey of Old Testament Introduction*, rev. ed. (Chicago: Moody, 1980), 440-445.

20. Davidic authorship vis-à-vis authenticity of headings is the subject of much debate, particularly because the "of" in "Of David" is an ambiguous preposition in the Hebrew. Actually it is just *one letter*, that is, one Hebrew consonant. It can mean "to," "about" or "by." But it is now generally held that the preposition (le) has genitive (or ownership) force and that the Septuagint rendition *tou David* ("of David") is more accurate. See James Arthur Mays, *Psalms: Interpretation: A Commentary for Teaching and Preaching* (Louisville: Westminster John Knox, 2011), 4-5, for how this applies to Psalm 3.

21. I understand that this exercise has limitations. In Chapter 10, I explain how psalm titles only point you in the right direction.

CHAPTER 3: PSALMS AS LITERATURE

22. New Testament writers typically quote from the Greek (Septuagint or LXX) and not from the original Hebrew Old Testament. Thus, when reading psalm citations in the New Testament, we are reading a *translation of a translation* (e.g., quotes in the Letter to the Hebrews).

23. Peter Craigie, "Psalms 1-50," *Word Biblical Commentary* (Dallas: Word Publishing, 1983), 25.

24. A word needs to be said here about terminology. Among commentaries, scholars do not use standard terminology. Some prefer to equate a "line" with a "colon." Others call a colon a "stich" and a bicolon a "dystich."

25. Some passages display a stair-like parallelism, consisting of several cola, each providing an element of the complete thought, as in Psalm 1:1. In climactic parallelism, the first line is repeated

and expanded to complete the thought, as in 29:1. In introverted parallelism, the first line is closely related in thought to the fourth, and the second to the third (chiastic), as in 91:14.

26. This is related to the notion of synthesis in parallelism. Some scholars teach that all parallel cola build upon the first. Because the movement from one cola to the next makes for a fuller thought, the message delivered by the entire line is a synthesis. This is a departure from the traditional understanding of the three basic kinds of parallelism which I've mentioned (synonymous, antithetic, synthetic). Scholars vary in their treatment of this subject. For further study, see Mark Futato, *Interpreting the Psalms* (Grand Rapids: Kregel Publications, 2007), 37-39, and Robert Alter, *The Art of Biblical Poetry* (N.Y.: Basic Books, 1985), 22ff.

27. Futato, 39-40.

28. Ibid.

29. Leland Ryken, *How to Read the Bible As Literature* (Grand Rapids: Zondervan, 1984), 89-90.

30. For further study, you may find helpful E. W. Bullinger, *Figures of Speech Used in the Bible* (Grand Rapids: Baker, 1968) and Milton S. Terry, *Biblical Hermeneutics* (1884; reprint, Grand Rapids: Zondervan, 1974).

31. As Walter Kaiser points out, "Figures of speech are not as precise in their meanings as prose is. What these figures lack in precision, however, is surely made up for in their increased ability to draw pictures for us and to give a vividness that ordinary prose cannot. In this way, our attention is drawn to certain items that otherwise might have been passed over." Walter C. Kaiser and Moises Silva, *Introduction to Biblical Hermeneutics* (Grand Rapids, MI: Zondervan, 1994), 98.

CHAPTER 4: THE TYPES OF PSALMS

32. They demonstrated the importance of what is called *form criticism*.

33. Along with another scholar, his student Joachim Begrich, he identified hymns, communal laments, complaints (individual laments), royal psalms, and individual thanksgiving psalms. Gunkel also gives some minor types. In this book, I have tended to follow Gunkel's classification (and most follow his in broad terms), but with modification based on Claus Westermann's work.

34. Gunkel's and Mowinckel's conclusions based on form-criticism were taken and refined by such scholars as H. Joachim-Kraus and

Claus Westermann. But the significance of form never left the discussion. See Tremper Longman III, "Lament," in *Cracking Old Testament Codes: A Guide to Interpreting the Literary Genres of the Old Testament*, edited by D. Brent Sandy and Ronald L. Giese (Nashville: Broadman and Holman, 1995), 197-216, and Claus Westermann, *Praise and Lament in the Psalms* (Atlanta: John Knox, 1981).

35. One fundamental observation relates the form of a psalm with its function, the purpose for which the psalm was written. In psalmody, function tends to shape the psalm; compositions with similar purposes took on similar structures. This observation holds true with other literary works from the Ancient Near East.

36. An individual praise psalm (18, 30, 40) is offered by an individual worshipper rather than a group. It usually includes a report on God's deliverance and a personal vow to render praise to God. On the other hand, a communal or national praise psalm (124, 129) reports that God has acted on behalf of the community. It is usually in response to a specific event that has just occurred. Others however would use a different scheme: psalms of descriptive praise cf. psalms of declarative praise. Robert Hughes and J. Carl Laney, *New Bible Companion* (Wheaton, IL: Tyndale, 1990), 234.

37. Estes, 184.

38. The *Hallel* psalms are found in three separate collections: the "Egyptian Hallel" (113-118), the "Great Hallel" (120-136), and the concluding Hallel psalms (146-150).

39. Other variations exist. There are royal laments (144:1-11) as well as royal thanksgiving songs (18, 118). In some royal psalms the king is the speaker (101), in others he is the spotlight of comment (45; 110).

40. Mowinckel, 118-129. Eaton, 65.

41. There is no consensus on how these psalms are to be classified, especially with regard to their form and original life setting. It is difficult to totally dismiss the didactic (teaching) dimension in these psalms. Many scholars would agree that the following are wisdom psalms: 1, 34, 37, 112. Crenshaw, 187ff.

42. Some associate them with Israel's pilgrimage from Exodus to Canaan. Others, with greater probability, connect them to Israelites "going up" (ascent) to Jerusalem to observe the annual feasts.

43. Intercessory psalms hold many parallels to the Psalms of Zion in that they communicate great concern for the Holy City and its residents. Often, they enumerate the kinds of help or support needed by the community, such as provisions, a bountiful harvest, or victory over opposition.

CHAPTER 5: THE GOD OF THE PSALMISTS

44. Driver, 368.

45. One outstanding feature of the Solomonic Temple is that there was no idol in it, having only the mercy seat over the Ark and the Cherubim overshadowing the former, declaring to the world that idols are unnecessary to define the presence of God or his sanctity.

46. The psalms speak about Jesus (Luke 24:44), the Messianic King. He exemplifies God's reign. And since he is the ultimate realization of the psalms, Jesus preached the Kingdom of God that was anticipated by the psalms. He even began his sermon on Kingdom Ethic with the word "blessed" (Matthew 5-7).

47. William L. Holladay, ed., *Concise Hebrew and Aramaic Lexicon of the Old Testament*, hereafter referred to as *CHALOT* (Grand Rapids, MI: Eerdmans, 1988), 326. Cf. *NIBD*, s.v. "horn." See also Deuteronomy 33:17 and Psalm 22:21.

48. Throughout Psalms, an assortment of Hebrew words may be translated "strength." These words are invariably associated with divine power, implying that God gives of his own strength. God is called "my strength" (18:1, 2; 19:14; 22:19; 28:7; 31:4; 43:2; 59:17; 118:14; 144:1) and "our strength" (46:1; 81:1). The psalmists also refer to him as "The strength of my life" (27:1), "The strength of my heart" (73:26), and "The strength of my salvation" (140:7).

49. Psalms 7:17; 9:2; 21:7; 46:4; 47:2; 50:14; 56:2; 57:2; 73:11; 77:10; 78:17; 78:56; 82:6; 83:18; 91:1, 9; 92:1; 107:11.

50. Refuge (9:9; 14:6; 46:7, 11; 48:3; 57:1; 59:16; 62:7; 62:8; 91:2, 9; 94:22; 104:18; 142:5), My/our defense (59:9, 16, 17; 62:6; 89:18; 94:22), My fortress (18:2; 31:3; 71:3; 91:2; 144:2), My salvation (27:1; 38:22; 51:14; 62:1, 2, 6; 88:1; 118:14, 21), A helper (30:10; 33:20; 54:4; 115:9). Walter Brueggemann, *Spirituality of the Psalms* (Minneapolis: Fortress Press, 2002), 53-54.

51. God is worshiped in his sanctuary because he has set his name there. He is the God whom the heavens cannot contain (1 Kings 8:27). He will hear in heaven the prayer which is offered toward the Temple as well as the prayer and praise in the Temple itself. Iain W. Provan, "1 and 2 Kings," *New International Biblical Commentary* (Peabody, MA: Hendrickson Publishers, 1995), 12ff.

52. The regularity of singing in Tabernacle worship one cannot determine. David, however, gave a new place to music, as may be seen already in the procession which brought up the Ark (2 Samuel 6:5). Craigie, 26.

53. There was evidently a "service of song" as described in The First Book of Chronicles (1 Chronicles 16, cf. Psalm 105:1-22; 96). William Smith, *Old Testament History*, 11 ed. (Joplin, Missouri: College Press, 1967), 472.

54. These songs may be seen as a subcategory of praise psalms or a variation of royal psalms. Zion or Jerusalem becomes the focal point of Israel's praise because God's favor rests there. See Chapter 9.

55. The divine indwelling of the Temple was symbolized by the Shekinah glory cloud which filled the house (1 Kings 8:10ff).

CHAPTER 6: EXTENSIVE THEMES IN PSALMS

56. Jesus launched his Sermon on the Mount in a similar way as Psalm 1, with beatitudes (Matthew 5:3ff). The Hebrew noun *ashriym* is an abstract plural. The word often refers to the happiness that derives from security and abundance with God (1:1, 3; 2:12; 34:9; 41:1; 65:4; 84:12; 89:15; 106:3; 112:1; 127:5; 128:1; 144:15). On occasion, it refers to the relief that one experiences when one's sins are forgiven.

57. I recommend a study of the "tree of life" image in the wisdom tradition (Proverbs 3:18, 11:30, 13:12, 15:4). Futato, 64.

58. *CHALOT*, 388.

59. See Proverbs 1:8, 3:1, 4:2, 6:20, and 7:2. Futato, 60.

60. Hebrew poetry is commonly associated with teaching wisdom. Jewish scholars classify Proverbs, Job, and Ecclesiastes as "wisdom literature." Many psalms or verses within psalms fit the category as well in terms of literary structures, vocabulary, and concepts. They frequently deal with topics such as the injustices of life and the justice of God, the responsibilities of proper living, and the transitory nature of human existence. Kevin J. Vanhoozer, ed. *Theological Interpretation of the Old Testament* (Grand Rapids, MI: Baker Books, 2008), 157.

61. Consider the psalmist's musings in Psalm 34 (NET): Turn away from evil and do what is right! Strive for peace and promote it! (v 14); Evil people self-destruct; those who hate the godly are punished (v 21). Note how — despite the psalmist's internal struggle — there is a decided leaning towards righteousness.

62. As G. Archer observes, "Whereas Greek philosophy tended toward dialectical deduction from first principles arrived at by purely intellectual induction, Hebrew philosophy was more intuitive and analogical, endeavoring to interpret the moral order in the light of a personal, omniscient, and omnipotent God, who had revealed his will for ethical living." Archer, 479.

63. Psalm 7:1, 9:9, 11:1, 14:6, 18:2, 18:30, 31:1-4, 36:7, 46:1, 59:16, 62:7-8, 64:10, 91:4, 91:9.

64. Futato, 99-100. At times, the psalmist will also combine one or more similar metaphors in a single verse (18:2, 62:7, 94:22, as well as 2 Samuel 22:3). This is typical of Davidic psalms.

CHAPTER 7: JESUS IN THE PSALMS

65. While the portrait details may not have been clear, nor cultural interpretation exact, what was evident was that they were seeking a messiah who would offer peace, redemption, and sovereign rule. Brueggemann, 10-11.

66. Also alluded to in Jesus' prayer for Jerusalem (Luke 13:35).

67. Willem A. Van Gemeren, "Psalms," ZNBC.

68. Christian-minded scholars are fairly agreed on seventeen specifically messianic psalms. These psalms, in the whole or in parts, refer to Christ in the third person (8:4-8; 72:6-17; 89:3-4, 28-29, 34-36; 109:6-19; 118:22; 132:11-12), address him in the second person (45:6-7; 68:18; 102:25-27; 110), or feature him speaking in the first person (2; 16:10, 22; 40:6-8; 41:9; 69:4, 21, 25; 78:2). *NIBD*, s.v. "Book of Psalms."

69. For instance, the titles for Jesus at the beginning of Mark's gospel are the ones found in Psalm 2. Vanhoozer, 158, 166.

70. E. Calvin Beisner, *Psalms of Promise* (Colorado Springs: NavPress, 1988), 246.

71. Eusebius calls Psalm 22 "a prophecy of the passion of Christ." For further study on related Christology, see N. T. Wright, *How God Became King: The Forgotten Story of the Gospels* (San Francisco, CA: Harper Collins, 2012) and John Durham, "The King As "messiah" in the Psalms." *Review and Expositor* 81 (1984).

CHAPTER 8: PSALMS AS LIFE-TOOLS

72. Henri Nouwen, *The Wounded Healer* (N.Y.: Image, 1979), 51-70.

73. Eugene H. Peterson, *Answering God: The Psalms as Tools for Prayer*, paperback ed. (San Francisco: Harper Collins, 1991), 12, 42, emphasis mine.

74. Interestingly, psalmists are as unguarded with their praise as they are with their complaints. This goes to show that total honesty with God was not a problem for them. This should inspire us to be the same.

75. Of course, there is no guarantee that just *any* prayer will lead to God. As Dietrich Bonhoeffer points out, "Prayer does not mean

simply to pour out one's heart. It means rather to find the way to God and to speak with him, whether the heart is full or empty. No man can do that by himself. For that he needs Jesus Christ. Dietrich Bonhoeffer, *Psalms: The Prayer Book of the Bible* (Minneapolis, MN: Augsburg Fortress Publishers, 1974), 9-10.

76. Warren W. Wiersbe, *The Wiersbe Bible Commentary: New Testament* (Colorado Springs: David Cook, 2007; originally printed as *The Bible Exposition Commentary* by Victor Books, 2003), 148.

77. Kaiser and Silva, 168-169.

78. Futato, 68.

79. Solutions come from thinking and doing (not just feelings). Popular counselling therapies tend to revolve around feelings. However, feelings don't immediately bring solutions. Neither are they the final arbiter of truth. On the other hand, *directed* feelings generate meaningful decisions. The psalms are instrumental in this regard.

80. Brueggemann, 34.

81. Kaiser and Silva, 169. Vanhoozer, 166.

82. James Crenshaw, *Old Testament Wisdom: An Introduction*, 3d ed. (Louisville, KY: Westminster, 2010), 188.

83. Miroslav Volf, *Exclusion and Embrace* (Nashville, TN: Abingdon Press, 1996), 123.

84. Walter C. Kaiser, Peter H. Davids, F.F. Bruce, Manfred T. Brauch, *Hard Sayings of the Bible*, hereafter referred to as *Hard Sayings* (Downers Grove, IL: Intervarsity Press, 1996), 280.

85. *Hard Sayings*, 282.

86. In some cases, there seems to be a belief that the psalmist (or Israel which he represents) is to be *the* instrument of justice or punishment (see 149:6-9). But even in these passages there is a sense that God has the final say in how things play out.

87. It's like pleading before a judge. They are "appeals to God to pour out His wrath upon the psalmist's enemies." Archer, 452.

88. The Exodus event is still in their minds. See Geoffrey Grogan, *Psalms* (Grand Rapids: Eerdmanns, 2008), 256-258.

89. *Hard Sayings*, 281.

90. Andrew Hill and John Walton, *A Survey of the Old Testament*, 2d ed. (Grand Rapids: Zondervan, 2000), 352.

91. What is called for is just *retribution*. This is often wished or portrayed as active judgment in which enemies will experience the harm that they had *intended* to inflict (5:10; 7:15; 10:2; 28:4; 35:7-8; 26; 79:12; 109:2-29).

92. *Hard Sayings*, 282.

93. Take Psalm 69 where David prays, "Pour out your wrath on them, and let your fierce anger overtake them" (69:24). The apostle Paul quotes this imprecation in Romans 11:9-10 as having Old Testament authority.

94. Claus Westermann, *Praise and Lament in the Psalms* (Atlanta: John Knox, 1981). Employing the Hebrew word for "thanks," he uses the term lament-*todah*-hymn.

95. In addition, the idea that the Psalms are connected (that is, praise at the end of one psalm may lead to a new concern in the next psalm/s) is a possible illustration that doxology is not the "end" of faith in God or Christian living, but part of the process of life. For A. Weiser, this phenomenon of transition is still about "union with God." Weiser, 15.

96. Westermann goes further to explore the elements of praise in all the psalms, proposing that the psalms are simply different modes of praise. Laments may be seen as "petitionary praise," anticipating that God will act. Next, "declarative praise" finds expression in thanksgiving psalms, seeing that God has acted. And finally, hymns extol God for who he is—"descriptive praise."

97. Vanhoozer, 162.

98. An ancient drama tradition in East Asia features a theater with two levels. The audience sees both levels. The *human* characters acting in the lower level "do not see" what goes on in the upper level, where the gods are presumed to be. As the plot unfolds, the viewers see the disconnection between the two "worlds." It is only when human characters from "below" gain perspective "from above" that the story is brought to resolution. Such is the effect of prayer. We acquire God's point of view.

99. Gene Edwards, *Crucified by Christians* (Sargent, GA: The Seed-Sowers, 1994), 13.

100. Ibid.

CHAPTER 9: A LIFE OF PRAISE

101. Walter W. Skeat, *An Etymological Dictionary of the English Language*, unabridged ed. (Mineola, NY: Dover, 2005), 469.

102. Specifically, in the *piel, pual,* and *hitpael* forms. Derivatives of this word (*hillul, mahalal, tehillah*) are also translated "praise." Usage denotes a joy in recognizing God's great qualities. *CHALOT*, 80-81.

103. The psalms praise God for "the totality of his dealings with men and of his being." Daniel J. Estes, *Handbook on the Wisdom Books*

and the Psalms (Grand Rapids, MI: Baker Books, 2005), 156.

104. The psalms were collectively called *sepher tehillim*, meaning "book of praises." Scholars point out that *tehillah* (singular of *tehillim*) denotes "praise-song" and that essentially, a psalm is a song of praise. This is a fitting description, considering that most psalms include some element of praise to God.

105. The psalmists insist that God ordained his covenant (111:9) and purposely recalls it (50: 5; 105:8; 106:45, 111:5). Blessing is promised for those who keep his covenant (103:18). This is in contrast to those who go forget or go against it (78:37; 44:17).

106. Peterson, 126-127. Peterson adds, "There is more. Psalm 150 does not stand alone; four more hallelujah psalms are inserted in front of it so that it becomes the fifth of five psalms that conclude the Psalter – five hallelujah psalms, one for each "book" of the Psalms, and the last, the 150th doing double duty as the conclusion to both the fifth book and to the five books all together."

107. Psalm 8:2b is "ordained praise" (NIV) or "founded a bulwark" (NRSV). However you translate, there is the idea that spoken praise is powerful; it subdues the enemies.

108. *ZNBC*, s.v. "Psalm 2." See how Jesus uses this passage to rebut religious leaders in Matthew 21:14-17.

109. It is not surprising that many psalms repeat some refrain about God or how he relates to people. Psalm 118 features the recurrent "His love endures forever."

CHAPTER 10: HOW TO STUDY INDIVIDUAL PSALMS

110. I mentioned earlier that the psalms abound with patterns—alliteration, assonance, word plays and acrostics, which are all but impossible to spot unless reading them in their original Hebrew.

111. It goes without saying that you will need a Bible. If you have several on hand, better. You will notice that although I have primarily used the New International Version (NIV), other translations were also cited. The NIV is a good dynamic equivalence (thought-for-thought) translation but for more serious Bible study I would include more literal (less interpretative) translations such as the NASB, ESV, and the NKJV.

112. For more on the titles, see Bullock, 24-30.

113. Besides, 42:5 is also found in 42:11 and 43:5 which leads some to suggest that the two psalms were originally one.

114. Gordon Fee and Douglas Stuart, *How to Read the Bible Book by*

Book, reprint ed. (Manila: OMF, 2003, orig. Grand Rapids: Zondervan, 2002), 134-143.

115. The effect is somewhat like studying the synoptic gospels (Matthew, Mark, Luke) in parallel. The same underlying convictions hold, but the emphases vary.

116. Futato, 29.

117. As Elmer Leslie states, "The psalm itself and its interpretation are in each case so interwoven that the experience which the psalm embodies unfolds before one's eyes." Elmer A. Leslie, *The Psalms, Translated and Interpreted in the Light of Hebrew Life and Worship* (New York: Abingdon-Cokesbury Press, 1949), 8.

118. Ryken, 91. This includes a better understanding of figurative language.

119. And now that I've mentioned Bible helps, here are two books that would be good additions to your library: G.B. Caird, *The Language and Imagery of the Bible* (Philadelphia: Westminster, 1980) and E. W. Bullinger, *Figures of Speech Used in the Bible* (Grand Rapids: Baker, 1968).

120. Peterson, 47.

121. I write this with caution, for we should not "read too much" into a psalm. For example, some read the psalms as doctrinal treatises, as if these inspired poems were intended to support the tenets of systematic theology.

122. The Hebrew word *nechilot* occurs only here, and the meaning is uncertain. It is probably related to *chalil*, a reed-instrument, hence "flutes." *CHALOT*, 223. In Bible times, it was not uncommon for poetry reading to be accompanied by a variety of instruments.

123. John W. Baigent and Leslie C. Allen, "The Psalms," *New International Bible Commentary*, F. F. Bruce, ed. (n.c.: Pickering and Inglis Ltd., 1979; Pradis Electronic Version produced by Zondervan Interactive, 2002).

124. The Hebrew literally reads, "The heart of them is destruction."

All of Rolan Monje's books are available at
www.ipibooks.com